The French Revolution

A Beginner's Guide

ONEWORLD BEGINNER'S GUIDES combine an original, inventive, and engaging approach with expert analysis on subjects ranging from art and history to religion and politics, and everything in between. Innovative and affordable, books in the series are perfect for anyone curious about the way the world works and the big ideas of our time.

anarchism

artificial intelligence

the beat generation

biodiversity

bioterror & biowarfare

the brain

the buddha

censorship

christianity

civil liberties

classical music

cloning

cold war

crimes against humanity

criminal psychology

critical thinking

daoism

democracy

dyslexia

energy

engineering

evolution

evolutionary psychology

existentialism

fair trade

feminism

forensic science

french revolution

history of science

humanism

islamic philosophy

journalism

lacan

life in the universe

machiavelli

mafia & organized crime

marx

medieval philosophy

middle east

NATO

oil

the palestine–israeli conflict

philosophy of mind

philosophy of religion

philosophy of science

postmodernism

psychology

quantum physics

the qur'an

racism

the small arms trade

sufism

The French Revolution
A Beginner's Guide

Peter Davies

ONEWORLD
OXFORD

A Oneworld Paperback Original

Published by Oneworld Publications 2009

Copyright © Peter J. Davies 2009

ISBN 978–1–85168–693–3

Typeset by Jayvee, Trivandrum, India
Cover design by Simon McFadden
Printed and bound in Great Britain by TJ International, Padstow

Oneworld Publications
185 Banbury Road
Oxford OX2 7AR
England
www.oneworld-publications.com

Learn more about Oneworld. Join our mailing list to
find out about our latest titles and special offers at:

www.oneworld-publications.com

Mixed Sources
Product group from well-managed
forests and other controlled sources
www.fsc.org Cert no. SGS-COC-2482
© 1996 Forest Stewardship Council

This book is dedicated to Emily and Leo

Contents

Acknowledgements

I would like to thank Fiona Slater and Marsha Filion at Oneworld for inviting me to write this book and Dawn Sackett and Isobel Brooks for their comments on the manuscript.

Introduction

The French made, in 1789, the greatest effort that has ever been made by any people to sever their history into two parts so to speak, and to tear open a gulf between their past and their future. In this design, they took the greatest care to leave every trace of their past condition behind them; they imposed all kinds of restraints upon themselves in order to be different from their ancestry; they omitted nothing which could disguise them. I have always fancied that they were less successful in this enterprise than has been generally believed abroad, or even supposed at home.

Alexis de Tocqueville

The main aim of this book is to provide readers with an accessible introduction to the French Revolution. It will offer an overview of events and blend narrative with analysis. I will contextualise the revolution in terms of what preceded it (the Old Regime), what followed it (the Napoleonic Empire), and how historians have interpreted it. This will allow an examination of the ideas and ideologies that underpinned the revolution – on the left and right – in a neutral and non-partisan way; analysing both the revolution and the Counter Revolution and bringing the story of the revolution up to date, by considering the legacy of the event and how it is still relevant in French political life today.

The revolution was a unique event. It lasted a decade and incorporated a number of phases and regimes. However, the idea that it was one revolution – singular, uniform and homogenous – needs examining. In reality, as this volume will demonstrate, it was actually a collection of distinct but overlapping revolts. And historians can look at them through a variety of different prisms, whether social, economic or political.

As an event, the revolution remains complex and fascinating. In France today it is a key reference point and major source of controversy. Every generation of historians has different theories and perspectives on the revolutionary decade and in the early years of the twenty-first century the level of scholarly interest shows no sign of diminishing. In addition, politicians talk about the rights of man, tourism websites highlight landmarks such as the Bastille and the Tuileries, and ordinary people still argue over dinner about the pros and cons of 1789. It would appear that the Bicentenary – celebrated in 1989 – merely increased awareness of the event and its significance.

The structure of the book is broadly chronological. In chapter 1 I will consider the nature of the Old Regime. What were its main characteristics and features? And how was it justified from within? This will lead into an examination of how and why the revolution occurred in chapter 2. Here I will assess a number of theories: that the revolution was caused by enlightened ideas, by a crisis of the monarchy, by the ambitious manoeuvrings of the Third Estate (and, in particular, its middle-class leadership).

The following two chapters will evaluate the early revolution. Chapter 3 will focus on the various revolts of 1789 – their character and significance; while chapter 4 will assess the liberal and constitutional phase of the revolution, 1790–92. The radicalisation of the revolution will be covered in chapter 5. Here the major historical debates are: Why did France go to war? How can we rationalise the Terror? And what was the relationship between revolutionary war and terror?

Thereafter, I look in other directions. In chapter 6 I shift the focus to the Counter Revolution. What forces opposed the revolution and how successful were they? In this section I am particularly interested in groups and individuals and their different approaches to combating the revolution. I then consider the post-Terror period. What did the Thermidorian Reaction (1794–95) mean for the revolution? And what were the aims and objectives of the Directory (1795–99)?

This brings me to the end of the revolutionary decade, but the aftermath and legacy of the revolution are also important. In chapter 9 I survey the revolutionary historiography through liberal, conservative, Marxist and revisionist phases. And in chapter 10 I measure the impact of the revolution today. In what ways does it resonate still?

A wide range of historical sources have been consulted. In each chapter I refer to key primary documents with the aim of adding texture and bringing the event alive. The main discussion is also situated against the backdrop of historical debate. Throughout, the ideas and theories of historians and secondary writers have been used to add context.

1

The Old Regime

In France, the three Estates have their order and rank one after the other, the ecclesiastical order being first, followed by the nobility, and the Third Estate last. This is true even though there are no statutes to this effect, because laws are scarcely made in matters simply of honour.

Charles Loyseau, 1666

There was no inevitability about the French Revolution. The Old Regime had existed and survived for many centuries. It had been accepted and respected and ordinary people had been reasonably content. Of course, in the 1780s the mood turned slightly and there was a feeling that change and revolution could happen. But we should not assume that this atmosphere pre-dated the 1780s to any great extent.

What was the *Ancien Régime*? The term translates as 'Old Kingdom', 'Old Rule' or, literally, 'Old Regime'. After 1789, the term came to be applied retrospectively to the arrangements associated with the previous system of absolute government. Here I will explore the meaning and significance of the Old Regime as an era. Its main pillars will also come under the spotlight: the estates system, the King and monarchy, and the provincial parliaments – *parlements*.

A society of estates

A satirical print from 1789 depicts three men on a wagonette on their way to the opening of the Estates General. Each represents one of France's three estates. At the front sits a priest who is dressed in black and steering the vehicle onwards. He is focused on the task in hand and does not seem to be communicating with his two passengers. Seated directly behind him is an aristocrat, dressed in a red and blue gown and wearing an extravagant, flowery hat; he is also flourishing a sword. At the back of the wagonette stands a simple peasant, without a seat and looking slightly forlorn; he seems to have some kind of agricultural implement in his hand. The peasant is looking up to the aristocrat, but the aristocrat has his right arm outstretched, as if slightly ignoring the peasant.

The idea of a 'society of orders' was well entrenched in Old Regime France and many prints and paintings of the day took it as their subject. It was a simple social system that everyone understood and no-one questioned. From the image in question we can glean that the clergy (the First Estate) had an accepted position at the top of society; that the aristocracy (the Second Estate) had a cherished military role and were next in line; and that the peasantry (who made up the bulk of the Third Estate) were the workers and also slightly forgotten about.

This was one caricaturist's view of French society in 1789, but what was the reality? Medieval monarchs had divided the population of the country into three estates in order to form a representative body. This came to be known as the Estates General and the expectation was that the Crown would take key issues such as taxation to the forum. This rarely happened; but the point of significance is that society had been subdivided into three estates and this was to have serious ramifications later.

The First Estate comprised the clergy, around 130,000 of them. This made it the smallest estate. But on account of its responsibilities – looking after the moral and spiritual wellbeing of people – it could claim to be the estate that was closest to the King and God. According to Charles Loyseau, a renowned legal scholar who wrote *A Treatise on Orders* in 1610:

> In this Christian kingdom, we have bestowed on God's minis-
> ters the first rank of honour, rightly making the clergy (that is
> to say, the ecclesiastical order) the first of our three Estates of
> France … In nearly all the states of Christendom the clergy are
> similarly constituted as a distinct order, as in France, which has
> always been more Christian and has honoured the Church
> more than any other nation on earth.

In this period religion was the dominant force in society, and so
the First Estate had a privileged position – literally and
metaphorically. The Catholic Church was all enveloping. It
owned ten per cent of all land, was a major employer, controlled
education, carried much political weight, and dispensed patron-
age on a vast scale. It had also been unsettled by theological
disputes in the seventeenth and eighteenth centuries – in particular, the growth of Jansenism. This body of thought, associated
with the teaching of Cornelius Jansen, Bishop of Ypres, incorporated notions of predestination and original sin. Jesuits and
Jansenists clashed, and the latter were excommunicated from the
Church in the second decade of the eighteenth century.

Next was the Second Estate. There were around 200,000
nobles in France at this time and between them they owned
about a third of all land, with feudal rights over much of the rest.
Their powerbase was the provinces. They had feudal domains,
personal fiefdoms, and looked upon the *parlements* as a symbol of
their power and independence from Paris. In terms of rank,
members of the Second Estate ranged from simple gentlemen to
knights and princes; and like the clergy, they thrived on privilege.

The aristocracy were fiercely protective of their access to the
monarch. In the *parlements* and Assembly of Notables – which
met first in February 1787 and again in November 1788 – they
felt they had a right, and duty, to advise the King. They became
more and more vociferous in this. By 1788, the princes of the
blood were addressing the King in desperate language:

> Sire, the state is in peril. Your person is respected, the virtues
> of the monarch assure him of the nation's respect. But Sire, a
> revolution is brewing in the elements of government and is
> being brought about by rousing the people. Institutions thought
> to be sacred, through which the monarchy has flourished for so
> many centuries, are being questioned, seen as problems, or even
> disparaged as unjust.

The problem for the Second Estate was that, as his reign wore
on, Louis felt less and less inclined to listen to what it had to say.

The Third Estate wasn't an estate in the sense that the other
two were. It was simply everyone else, the other ninety-five
per cent of the population. At the top of the Third Estate were
the educated, professional and merchant classes. The eighteenth
century would be theirs; they would be at the forefront of an
industrial and commercial boom and this would ultimately
encourage their political ambitions. This bourgeoisie – to use
the term employed by Marxist historians – owned twenty-five
per cent of all land and at times almost merged into the aristocracy. Hence the phrase 'bourgeois living nobly'. Because the
Third Estate was so huge and diverse, there were going to be
divisions. The middle classes had little in common with ordinary
town dwellers and peasants, who comprised the vast majority of
the population (and of the Third Estate). There was little
outright antagonism, just a realisation that as social groups they
had differing aspirations and expectations.

By 1789 the Third Estate had its champions. In January,
Abbé Sieyès, the 'vicar-general' of Chartres, published a
pamphlet which was provocatively entitled *What is the Third
Estate?* In it he argued that the Third Estate was entitled to more
respect on account of its hard work and toil:

> It suffices here to have made it clear that the pretended utility
> of a privileged order for the public service is nothing more than
> a chimera; that with it all that which is burdensome in this

service is performed by the Third Estate; that without it the superior places would be infinitely better filled; that they naturally ought to be the lot and the recompense of ability and recognised services, and that if privileged persons have come to usurp all the lucrative and honourable posts, it is a hateful injustice to the rank and file of citizens and at the same a treason to the public. Who then shall dare to say that the Third Estate has not within itself all that is necessary for the formation of a complete nation? It is the strong and robust man who has one arm still shackled. If the privileged order should be abolished, the nation would be nothing less, but something more. Therefore, what is the Third Estate? Everything; but an everything shackled and oppressed. What would it be without the privileged order? Everything, but an everything free and flourishing. Nothing can succeed without it, everything would be infinitely better without the others.

There was an attack on the other, 'non-productive' estates and a heartfelt plea for recognition and improved representation. It was this publication, and others like it, that helped to create an atmosphere in which political change was mooted.

Notwithstanding the new and obvious ambition of the Third Estate, French society had remained pretty static for centuries. Both nobles and peasants had bought into the feudal idea and the reciprocal obligations that it entailed. Land was the main currency. It is what the nobility owned and the peasantry worked. France was a large, predominantly agricultural country and this dynamic – between lord and vassal – was fundamental to the way that society operated.

King and monarchy

The King stood at the apex of the feudal system. He was a father figure, slightly aloof and detached, but accepted and, for much of the time, loved as France's natural leader. He personified a political system that based itself on concepts such as succession and delegation, and ordinary people were 'subjects' and nothing more. Doyle says that French kings did not require coronations because they were divine and ruled by the grace of God. Shennan argues that the King was absolute rather than despotic and ruled in accordance with both God and the law – with the key point being that a true despot would not take account of the law.

In 1787, Chrétien-François de Lamoignon, Keeper of the Seals, spoke for the King at the Paris parliament. For him, 'The principles of the French Monarchy' were:

> that the King alone must possess the sovereign power in his kingdom; that He is answerable only to God in the exercise of his power; that the tie which binds the King to the Nation is by nature indissoluble; that the interests and reciprocal obligations between the King and his subjects serve only to reassure that union; that the Nation's interest is that the powers of its head not be altered; that the King is the chief sovereign of the Nation and everything he does is with her interests in mind; and that finally the legislative power resides in the person of the King independent of and unshared with all other powers.

These words were spoken in a specific context – the treasury wishing to borrow an extra 420 million *livres* – but the same sentiments could have been articulated in any decade of the preceding centuries.

French kings were absolute in the sense that, at a national level, they did not have to share power with a parliament, and the Estates General – the only body that could conceivably limit the power of the monarch – met infrequently to say the least (it had last been convened in 1614). But, however absolute they were in theory, monarchs did require some assistance. That is why they appointed *gouverneurs* and, later, *intendants* to look after day-to-day affairs in the provinces. As can be imagined, the individuals who worked for the King were anything but popular. The perception was that they were out of touch and arbitrary in their decision-making, and as a result they had to bear the brunt of local people's unhappiness.

The French royal family resided at Versailles where they were surrounded by friends, relatives and advisors. Court politics were notoriously complex with the monarch of the day having to adjudicate between competing factions and personalities. Would the monarch be strong enough to stand up to particularly noisy cliques? Or would he become their prisoner? This varied according to the personalities involved. What rarely changed was the perception of the Court as a place of extravagance and corruption; and in time it came to epitomise the need for reform.

The monarchs of France had acquired a sizeable empire. They had accrued territory in North America, the Caribbean, West Africa, India and the Indian Ocean. This brought added influence but also the potential for disagreements and conflict. During the eighteenth century, France was involved in many wars, including the War of the Spanish Succession, War of the Austrian Succession, Seven Years' War and American Revolutionary War. Some of these wars were as much about trade and empire as about disputed successions. In this era, warfare involved large standing armies, technically sophisticated weaponry and fortifications, as well as big, costly navies. Consequently, issues of taxation and finance were crucial to ministers and monarchs. If France was to be involved in a war, she would have to finance it through taxation or some other means, and this would often prove controversial.

For the most part, the monarchy ruled in amateurish fashion. This was nowhere better illustrated than in the realm of finance. Budgets, for example, were based on guesswork. And the background was not ideal. Louis XVI was heavily in debt; in fact, he was still paying off money spent by previous kings on foreign-policy expeditions. For this reason, taxation became the major issue of the day. It was not just a question of deciding on a rate. Basic questions also had to be asked, like: Who do we tax? Who gets exemptions? How do we collect the money? Needless to say, it was the Second Estate who felt most threatened when taxation was discussed.

Nevertheless, the monarchy was accepted. It had stood the test of time and there was no realistic alternative. But, by the last quarter of the eighteenth century, issues had started to emerge. Was the monarchy in slow decline? Was it able to reform itself? Was it simply too extravagant?

The cloud on the horizon was the aristocracy. They had a strange relationship with the monarchy. On account of their shared outlook and value system they were natural bedfellows. But they were also rivals. The aristocracy thrived on status and privilege and were opposed to any attempt to reform 'the system' and reduce their privileges and exemptions. For this reason they did not agree with the idea of absolutism, because an absolute king might use his unchecked power to undermine their position in society.

The King was aware of this and on occasions felt the need to remind the aristocrats, in their provincial *parlements*, of their subservient status. For example, in 1788, he stated:

> When I come to personally hold my Parlement it is because I wish to hear a discussion of the law that I have brought with me and to learn more about it before I decide on its registration. This is what I did ... I heard everyone's opinion. You only need summarise these opinions when I am not present at your deliberations, in which case I am aware of the result of your debates by knowing how the majority voted. When I am present, I will decide this for myself. If, in my courts, my will was subject to the majority vote, the monarchy would be

> nothing more than an aristocracy of magistrates, as adverse to the rights and interests of the nation as to those of the sovereign. Indeed, it would be a strange constitution that diminishes the will of the King to the point that it is worth no more than the opinion of one of his officers, and requires that legislators have as many opinions as there are different decisions arising from the various courts of law in the kingdom.

It was a battle of wits. Occasionally, the monarchy might demonstrate reforming intentions. In response, the aristocrats would fall back on their ancient 'rights' and 'liberties' and argue through the *parlements* that they had special immunity. In the end, they called for the convocation of the Estates General to protect their privileges, but couldn't forsee that this body would actually listen to calls for fairer representation and sound the death knell for Second Estate power and influence.

Law and the *parlements*

The head of the French legal system was the chancellor, who oversaw a complex network of lower and higher courts. The lower courts, such as tribunals and *prévôtés*, dealt with minor crimes and offences. The higher courts had much wider authority and their decisions could only be revoked by the King. Of crucial importance here were the *parlements*. They were royal courts of law which had both judicial and legislative functions. There were thirteen regional *parlements* in all and they were frequented by individuals of birth and money (the qualification for membership). Their powers were extensive and resided in three main areas: the law, politics and policing.

The Parliament of Paris was the most important. It had been established in 1307 out of the King's Council and was originally the only such body in the kingdom. It sat inside the medieval royal palace on the Ile de la Cité and accrued much prestige and power. It was highly protective of the institution of the monarchy and would try cases of parricide. Where there was a guilty verdict it would also hand out torture and punishments (which could take the form of the burning of hands and wholesale dismemberment).

The relationship between the Crown and the *parlements* was vital. Cobban argues that the *parlements* were strong when the monarchy was weak, but when the monarchy was powerful – under the rule of Louis XIV, for example – they rarely tried to challenge the monarch or, put more accurately, were never in a position to do so. There was little love lost between the *parlements* and the Crown. The relationship could be described as one of uneasy coexistence; each was slightly wary of the other. But only occasionally did this lack of trust emerge into the open.

It happened in 1766 during the 'Brittany Affair', when the King was forced to say:

> I shall not tolerate in my kingdom the formation of an association that would cause the natural bond of similar duties and common responsibilities to degenerate into a confederation for resistance, nor shall I tolerate the introduction into the monarchy of an imaginary body that could only upset its harmony. The magistracy does not form a body nor a separate order among the three orders of the kingdom. The magistrates are my officers, responsible for carrying out my royal duty of rendering justice to my subjects, a function that ties them to me personally and that will always render them praiseworthy in my eyes.

Four years later, in 1770, three new ministers – chancellor Maupeou, finance minister Terray and foreign minister d'Aguillon – confronted the *parlements* over their powers, and a year later, on 19 January 1771, Maupeou executed a coup which created a new system of 'superior courts'. His aim was to reassert the Crown's power over the provincial *parlements* and establish a more uniform judicial system. His actions attracted much criticism but Voltaire, for one, approved of his work.

And it also occurred in 1776, when, as a retort to Turgot's financial reforms, the Parliament of Paris stated:

> The desire to ease the burdens placed on the people is too praiseworthy in a sovereign and conforms so much with the wishes of your *parlement* that the latter could never conceive of dissuading Your Majesty from such a noble and legitimate goal. But when projects, with such pleasant prospects, lead to real and increased injustices and even imperil the constitution and the tranquility of the state, it is our faithful duty, without seeking to place obstacles in the way of your beneficence, to establish laws against the imprudent efforts being made to commit Your Majesty to a course of action whose pitfalls and dangers have been concealed from you.

This was the crux of the matter. The *parlements* were of an independent mindset and were not afraid to flex their muscles. Their perception of themselves was interesting. They wished to be viewed as one of the bulwarks of the Old Regime, as a kind of 'barrier' that those in Paris had to contend with. They put enormous emphasis on the protection of feudal rights. This was their primary mission: to guard the vestiges of traditional society and keep the monarchy in check whenever it looked as if the king of the day was entertaining notions of reform.

In this sense, somewhat by default, the *parlements* were loyal to the idea of constitutional, rather than absolute, monarchy. A constitutional king, they (perhaps mistakenly) believed, would defer to the *parlements* and grant them a key role in protecting what they saw as 'constitutional principles'; whereas, an absolute monarch would simply sidestep them. Somewhat bizarrely

perhaps – given their elevated view of themselves – the
parlements also looked to the people for support. This is what
happened in the 1780s when the *parlements* called for the Estates
General to be convoked. Unfortunately, though, on this
occasion, the people were not interested in supporting the
parlements and used the convocation of the Estates General to put
in motion what turned out to be revolutionary demands.

In the words of Cobban, the ideology of the *parlements* was
akin to the 'conservatism of a close professional oligarchy'. For
Aulard, the *parlements* were instrumental in bringing some kind
of revolution closer because they stopped the monarchy from
evolving and reforming its institutions.

Assessments of the *Ancien Régime*

Historians of the French Revolution have paid close attention to
the Old Regime. Sutherland has enquired into the various crises
of the monarchy. His argument is that a pattern started to
develop: the Crown needed money for a special project, it
increased taxes accordingly, and then had to deal with criticism
and questioning. He focuses on one crisis in particular, that
which coincided with the Seven Years War (1756–63). He
relates how 'the government doubled the *vingtième* [income tax]
in 1756, and tripled it in 1760' but also had to listen as magistrates in the *parlements* spoke 'for everyone … who was affected,
privileged or not, or for all those haunted by the nightmare of
unchecked fiscality devouring the wealth of the nation'.

Lefebvre, looking at the issue from a Marxist perspective,
focuses on class. 'The history of the Capetian monarchy had in
fact been the story of its struggle against the aristocracy,' he
wrote. 'Sometimes the royal power had won out, as under
Francis I and Henry II … Sometimes the aristocracy had regained
the advantage, through the wars of religion, the minority of

Louis XIII or the Fronde.' Doyle, meanwhile, considers the position of ordinary folk under the Old Regime. He says, 'Poverty was France's most visible social problem. Nobody could overlook it. All travellers noticed the misery of rural housing and the poor appearance of the peasantry ... The poor, meaning those without adequate employment or other assured means of support, numbered at the best of times almost a third of the population.' Recent studies of the Old Regime, such as Peter Campbell's *Power and Politics in Old Regime France, 1720–1745*, have stressed the hegemonic role played by the aristocracy and have also focused on peculiar aspects of the pre-1789 system, such as factionalism and political management.

At the time, when the Old Regime (or what would come to be known as the Old Regime) was at its strongest, it was accepted as something that was natural and organic. This belief was widespread and rarely needed articulating. One man who attempted this was Loyseau, a lawyer at the Parlement of Paris. 'It is necessary that there be order in all things,' he wrote, 'for their well being and for their direction.' He went on to justify the way in which French society was regulated:

> Because we cannot live together in equality of condition, it is necessary that some command and others obey. Those who command have several orders, ranks, or degrees ... And the people, who obey all of the others, are themselves separated into several orders and ranks, so that over each of them there are superiors responsible for the whole order before the magistrates, and the magistrates to the sovereigns. Thus by means of these multiple divisions and subdivisions, the several orders make up a general order, and the several Estates a state well ruled, in which there is a good harmony and consonance, and a correspondence and interconnectedness from the highest to the lowest, in such a way that through order a numberless variety is led to unity.

Loyseau's language is reminiscent of that used by military commanders and Ancient Greek philosophers: the need for order, hierarchy and division of labour. There is also an assumption that 'equality of condition' is unrealisable; and we should note that even in the early period of the revolution there was little interest in this as a political goal (there were too many vested interests standing in the way).

2
Origins and causation

The abuses attending the levy of taxes were heavy and universal. The kingdom was parceled into generalities [administrative districts], with an intendant at the head of each, into whose hands the whole power of the crown was delegated for everything except the military authority; but particularly for all affairs of finance … The rolls of the *taille*, *capitation*, *vingtiemes*, and other taxes, were distributed among districts, parishes, and individuals, at the pleasure of the intendant, who could exempt, change, add, or diminish at pleasure. Such an enormous power, constantly acting, and from which no man was free, must, in the nature of things, degenerate in many cases into absolute tyranny.

Arthur Young

Narrative overview: financial and political problems

On 10 May 1774, Louis XVI acceded to the French throne, and thirteen months later, on 11 June 1775, he was crowned in Reims. During this period, France entered the War of American Independence (1778) and Jacques Necker, as director-general of the royal finances, published his analysis of the financial situation – the *Compte rendu au roi* (1781). This was a controversial document as, for the first time, the income and expenditure of the French government was made public. Necker was dismissed soon after – partly because of the stir his work had created and partly because of his unpopularity with Marie-Antoinette.

Necker was a crucial figure during the 1780s. Born in Geneva, he had made his name as a banker, establishing the Thellusson & Necker bank and also becoming a director of the French East India Company. He came to the attention of the French government on account of the money he was lending the monarchy and the lobbying activities of his wife. He was appointed director-general of royal finances on three separate occasions between 1771 and 1789 and became personally associated with plans to reform the taxation system and fund the national debt. He gained widespread popularity on account of his reforming ideas – in both economic and political spheres.

In 1783, the Vicomte de Calonne became controller-general and the Treaty of Versailles put an end to the American war. In 1785, the Queen, Marie Antoinette, was discredited by her involvement in the Diamond Necklace Affair. A member of the Court, Cardinal de Rohan, was under the impression that he could regain her favour by gifting her a valuable diamond-encrusted necklace. Secretly, the Queen had let it be known that she desired the necklace but when Rohan was unable to meet the cost of the first instalment, the jewellers went direct to the Queen for the necessary payment. The necklace somehow ended up in London and Rohan and his accomplices were exiled. Marie-Antoinette had done nothing wrong but the fallout from the affair did her few favours. It strengthened the image of her as a queen who was too closely associated with luxury and extravagance.

The following year, Calonne announced that the monarchy was insolvent. His proposed solution was to impose tax and fiscal reform on the aristocracy, while also reducing expenditure and encouraging free trade. It was against this background of financial difficulties that the Assembly of Notables met in 1787, and again in 1788. The Assembly was an enlarged version of the

King's Council, called to give him expert advice in times of crisis. Louis was hoping that the Assembly would support his reform programme but he and Calonne misjudged its mood and not even a compromise could be reached. (This impasse came against the backdrop of the Maupeou coup of 1771). This led to the demise of Calonne.

In April 1787, Loménie de Brienne was appointed chief minister and in May, the Assembly of Notables was dissolved. In June, Brienne published proposals for tax reform but on 2 July, the Parlement of Paris rejected these. This led to tension between the Crown and the *parlements*, which lasted into 1788. In August 1788, Brienne announced that the ancient Estates General would meet to discuss the prevailing financial and political situation. This was a major step and signified that France was in crisis. Necker succeeded Brienne and struck a conciliatory tone with those who had been critical of Brienne's time in power and on 6 November, he convoked a second Assembly of Notables to discuss the issue of the Estates General. But five weeks later, it was dismissed by Necker on account of its unsympathetic attitude to reform.

It was announced by Necker in December that the system of representation in the Estates General would be altered to give the Third Estate twice as much voting strength, to the obvious detriment of the First and Second estates' influence. This was the result of a number of factors: the voice of the Third Estate was becoming louder, the decisions that were being made at a local level (the provincial assembly in the Dauphiné, for example, had already voted to increase Third Estate representation), and a growing realisation in the corridors of government that a gesture had to be made. On 24 January 1789, the Estates General was convoked and met on 5 May, but with voting still by estate. By 27 June, the King had been forced into recognising the new National Assembly, with the estates having come together. The revolution was in motion.

Conspiracy, collapse or overthrow?

A traditional view is that the revolution originated in the radical ideas of the Enlightenment; according to this line of thought, the Old Regime was undermined by the *philosophes* and their demands for reform. Another perspective takes as its focus the monarchy and its problems during the 1770s and 1780s; the argument here is that the political system collapsed from within. By contrast, the Marxist view sees 1789 as a class revolution; the aspirational bourgeoisie were wanting more political power to add to their growing economic power.

The excerpt from Arthur Young's diaries quoted above offers us an alternative perspective on the issue. Young was an English traveller who happened to find himself in France as the revolution began to unfold. He had no ideology; he was simply a foreign observer who wrote about what he saw. For the most part, he focuses on economic and administrative matters, but the last line of the passage intimates that political issues might also have played their part.

In examining why the revolution occurred we must initially focus on two major undercurrents to the years 1787–89: the Aristocratic Revolution and the *cahiers de doléances*. The Aristocratic Revolution of 1787–89 was not a 'revolution' in the same sense that the revolutions of the middle classes, the people and the peasantry (in 1789) were 'revolutions'. In fact, it was not a revolution at all. That is why many authors now choose to use the phrase 'Aristocratic Reaction' instead. For the aristocrats concerned – mainly in the provinces but also in the capital – were wary of the King's reforming instincts and so 'revolted' or 'reacted' in an effort to halt his plans. At the heart of the Aristocratic Reaction were the Assembly of Notables and the Parliament of Paris, two bodies which were fiercely protective of aristocratic interests but which, ultimately, could not rescue the fortunes of the Second Estate.

The *cahiers de doléances* were a different matter. They were lists of grievances drawn up by members of all three estates to accompany the convocation of the Estates General in 1789. It was a primitive system but everyone was allowed to have their say: right across France, men and women, from the downtrodden peasant to the extravagant noble. It is impossible to summarise or synthesise the main ideas emanating from the *cahiers* because they were so diverse. But it is possible to give a flavour of them. An excerpt from a *cahier* from the First Estate declares:

> The clergy of the bailliage of Blois have never believed that the constitution needed reform. Nothing is wanting to assure the welfare of king and people except that the present constitution should be religiously and inviolably observed.

And from the Second Estate:

> Happiness ought not to be confined to a small number of men; it belongs to all. It is not an exclusive privilege to be contested for; it is a common right which must be preserved, which must be shared, and the public happiness is a source from which each has a right to draw his supply. Such are the sentiments which animate the nobility of the bailliage of Blois, at a moment when we are called upon by the sovereign to give our representatives to the nation. These principles have occupied all our thoughts during the preparation of this *cahier*. May they animate all citizens of this great state! May they evoke that spirit of union, that unanimity of desires which shall erect upon an indestructible foundation of power the prosperity of the nation, the welfare of the monarch and his subjects!

Crucially, where the Third Estate was concerned, the *cahiers* were a key barometer of morale. Is it possible to discern any

meaningful signs of revolution on the horizon in these *cahiers*?
By way of examples: at the lower end of the estate, we are told
of the 'unjust, onerous, and humiliating dues and other unheard
of burdens which the undersigned inhabitants of the seigneury
of Montjoye-Vaufrey are made to endure by the Count of
Montjoye-Vaufrey'; higher up there is the demand:

> That all the orders, already united by duty and a common desire
> to contribute equally to the needs of the State, also deliberate in
> common concerning its needs. That no citizen lose his liberty
> except according to law; that, consequently, no one be arrested
> by virtue of special orders, or, if imperative circumstances
> necessitate such orders, that the prisoner be handed over to the
> regular courts of justice within forty-eight hours at the latest.
> That no letters or writings intercepted in the post [mails] be the
> cause of the detention of any citizen, or be produced in court
> against him, except in case of conspiracy or undertaking against
> the State. That the property of all citizens be inviolable, and
> that no one be required to make sacrifice thereof for the public
> welfare, except upon assurance of indemnification based upon
> the statement of freely selected appraisers ... That every
> personal tax be abolished; that thus the *capitation* and the *taille*
> and its accessories be merged with the *vingtièmes* in a tax on land
> and real or nominal property. That such tax be borne equally,
> without distinction, by all classes of citizens and by all kinds of
> property, even feudal and contingent rights.

In this *cahier* alone we can see themes that would gain a profile
later, in the first months of the revolution: fairer representation,
the demand for liberty, the sanctity of property, equality of
taxation. In this sense, the *cahiers* are an illuminating guide to the
'state of the nation' in 1789. But the question remains: what
actually *caused* the revolution?

No debate has consumed historians more than the origins
and causation of the revolution. Was the outbreak of revolution

in 1789 related to Court politics, noble factions, the ideology of the *parlements*, army reform or foreign affairs? There is certainly evidence to suggest that these issues were of significance. But, to clarify matters we will look at three main perspectives on the revolution. Was it the result of an intellectual conspiracy? Or the failings of the King and monarchy? Or the ambitions of the middle classes?

The Enlightenment: 'high' and 'low'

The oldest theory of the revolution claims that it was an intellectual conspiracy, a product of enlightened thinking. During the eighteenth century a diverse group of thinkers took the lead in advancing a new type of philosophy. The Enlightenment stressed ideas such as individualism, harmony and tolerance. It also questioned the 'old certainties' of the past, such as religion and monarchy. The inference was that a truly enlightened society would base itself on rationalism – working things out in an almost scientific way – rather than tradition.

Among the key proponents of Enlightenment ideas were Rousseau, Voltaire and Montesquieu. They were educated individuals, from the upper echelons of society, and their work was read by members of the upper and upper-middle classes. The phrase 'High Enlightenment' has come to describe this phenomenon. This is to differentiate it from the 'Low Enlightenment', which, through the writings of Robert Darnton, has come to denote the work of journalists and scandal-mongers who wandered the streets of Paris looking for seedy gossip with the aim of destabilising the monarchy. The 'High' and 'Low' enlightenments had little in common – they were polar opposites in many respects – but together, unknowingly, they had the same enemy: the Old Regime, and the institution of the monarchy in particular.

Historians have exerted much energy debating the exact relationship between the Enlightenment and the revolution. But this is not a simple question. Can ideas cause political events? Was it simply a case of cause and effect? Or was it more complicated than that? The textbook view is that there is a simple causal relationship between the Enlightenment and the revolution: a body of ideas emerged which played a crucial role in undermining the institutions of the Old Regime. This argument has several key strands. Hampson sets the scene by stating that ideas are important in history and can be significant in the origins and causation of events. He identifies a realistic link between the influence of the Enlightenment and the post-1789 reorganisation of France, the end of the *parlements* and the abolition of the death penalty (that is, until the onset of the Terror).

Other historians suggest that Enlightenment ideas were shared by members of the middle class and the aristocracy; both, they argue, were opposed to the tax-increasing tendencies of the King's government. Likewise, de Tocqueville, writing in the nineteenth century, argued that the influence of the Enlightenment could be seen in the *cahiers*. He also argued that the *philosophes* (nobles themselves) filled the void left by the aristocracy.

It is problematic, but if we take individual thinkers we can, to some extent, trace their influence. Rousseau talked about the 'natural rights of man' and the 'social contract'; by the autumn of 1789 the revolutionary middle classes had put their seal on the *Declaration of the Rights of Man* and had also stated that individual men and women were *citoyens* rather than subjects of the King. Montesquieu articulated the theory of the 'separation of powers'; by 1791, the King had lost his power to dissolve the legislature and the law had become pre-eminent in all political matters.

But we must be clear. Individuals such as Rousseau and Montesquieu did not see themselves as radicals. Far from it in fact: they believed in reform rather than revolution and, as members of the aristocracy, were pillars of the establishment. Likewise, it could be argued that the Enlightenment wasn't *political* in any real sense, and that to see it as such would be to underestimate it. Its remit was much broader than that; it encompassed culture, society and religion as well as political ideas. And this breadth of scope would tend to minimise the impact the Enlightenment could have had on the political system.

Away from the orthodox view, there are other interpretations, most notably that which suggests that rather than inspiring the revolution, Enlightenment ideas actually spread on the back of the political changes. It has been argued that the new, emerging capitalist class, pleasantly surprised by the ease with which they achieved power, were in urgent need of philosophical support. And in the ideas of the Enlightenment they found a set of ideas and arguments that sat comfortably with their *raison d'être* as a class.

'Collapse': the crisis of the monarchy

Here the argument is that crisis in the 1770s and 1780s led to the collapse of the state in 1789. That is, crisis mixed with corruption and inequities. Arthur Young paints a depressing picture of France under Louis XVI:

> It must be obvious that the friends, acquaintances, and depen-
> dents of the *intendant*, and of all his *sub-delegues*, and the friends
> of these friends, to a long chain of dependence, might be
> favoured in taxation at the expense of their miserable neigh-
> bours; and that noblemen in favour at court, to whose protec-
> tion the *intendant* himself would naturally look up, could find
> little difficulty in throwing much of the weight of their taxes on

others, without a similar support. Instances, and even gross ones, have been reported to me in many parts of the kingdom, that made me shudder at the oppression to which [people have been subjected] by the undue favours granted to such crooked influence.

Later, historians of the revolution sided with this line of thinking. 'With the convening of the notables,' Furet wrote, 'the French monarchy had entered into the machinery of consultation: a strong government, a definite policy might have found support in that. But a weak and indecisive government risked exposing its isolation and hastening its own downfall; a single breach in the wall and a rout would ensue.' In another passage, he argued:

> The year 1788 ... saw the culmination of the old struggle which had begun after Louis XIV's death, between absolutist administration and *parlementaire* resistance. But it soon revealed to what extent the inequality of political forces had grown since Louis XVI's accession. Between a solitary and discredited monarchy, with nothing to offer but vague inclinations, and the great liberating watchword of the Estates General, uniting all ambitions, public feeling did not hesitate.

The crisis of the monarchy came to a head in the 1780s; there were difficulties in a number of areas and the result was a paralysing political situation. France was facing huge dilemmas in the area of finance. She faced an annual deficit of 100 million *livres*. Deficits were not unusual but in this particular case the monarchy had to decide between cutting costs, raising taxes, borrowing more money or actually going into bankruptcy. The situation was aggravated by a number of poor harvests in the 1770s and 1780s and an expanding population. The price of basic foodstuffs had to rise and because demand for this produce was, by definition, inelastic (there were no realistic alternatives), peasants began to show their displeasure by engaging in random acts of violence. Shennan argues that France was suffering for its conservative social and political attitudes and its inability or unwillingness to modernise and reform.

There were also tensions and problems in the sphere of government and kingship. To modernise or not? The instinct to reform was present – there was a yearning for more efficient and professional government. But at the same time, the monarchy had to be aware of the many vested interests at the heart of French society, and the aristocracy for one was determined to retain its special freedoms and privileges. The monarch himself was also an issue. He was not unpopular as a ruler but was only moderately talented and came to be noted for his indecisiveness. For these reasons, he could not be viewed in the same light as the 'Sun King', Louis XIV, against whom all monarchs judged themselves or were judged.

Under Louis XIV the kingdom had undergone administrative and financial reorganisation and trade and manufacturing were developed. The army was reformed and the period saw many military victories. Finally, Louis encouraged an extraordinary blossoming of culture encompassing theatre (Molière and Racine), music (Lully), architecture, painting, sculpture, and all the sciences (with the founding of the royal academies). During his reign Paris had become the centre of European politics. French had established itself as the language of diplomacy and the monarch himself had engaged in a range of glory-seeking enterprises.

In contrast, under Louis XVI, France lost her way slightly, particularly in the area of foreign policy. A case in point was the American War of Independence (1776–83). The King became embroiled in this conflict but it only had negative side-effects: the French national debt worsened and the achievements of the American colonists in the face of a European power seemed to encourage demands for reform in France.

So, it is hard to challenge the view which says that France was suffering from a multi-faceted crisis. The key issue was reform. The 'Royal Thesis' says that France in the 1780s was witnessing a confrontation between a reform-minded monarchy and a reactionary aristocracy. Louis was being influenced by Enlightenment ideas and saw the need for reform; the aristocracy interpreted this as the Crown being absolutist, being unaccountable to them, and trying to push through change against the wishes of others (i.e. themselves). And in an effort to protect their privileges they called for the convocation of the Estates General – a key development in the Aristocratic Reaction.

In the same vein, Egret has talked about a period of 'pre-revolution', a prolonged crisis of the monarchy in the period 1787–89. The main focus here is finance – and in particular the monarchy's financial deficit and debt – but we should be slightly suspicious of any label (e.g. 'pre-revolution') that is attached to an era in retrospect.

'Overthrow': the ambition of the Third Estate

Well before the advent of Marx and Marxism there were writers who wished to emphasise the power and significance of the Third Estate as a key factor in late-eighteenth-century politics. In fact, several months prior to the Tennis Court Oath and the Fall of the Bastille, Emmanuel-Joseph Sieyès had written about the position of the Third Estate in the French social structure. 'Public functions may be classified … under four recognised heads; the sword, the robe, the church and the administration,' he wrote. 'It would be superfluous to take them up one by one, for the purpose of showing that everywhere the Third Estate attends to nineteen-twentieths of them, with this distinction;

that it is laden with all that which is really painful, with all the burdens which the privileged classes refuse to carry. Do we give the Third Estate credit for this?'

This was one of many rhetorical questions posed by Sieyès in his pamphlet, *What is the Third Estate?* Almost without knowing, he was contributing to an atmosphere of questioning and disquiet. It is tempting to see Sieyès as some kind of John the Baptist figure, preparing the way for the revolution, but at the time the man himself would have viewed this idea as preposterous. He was an *abbé*, a man who had not been ordained as a priest. But he was a prominent administrator in the Catholic Church – in effect, the 'vicar-general' of the diocese of Chartres. And, in the wake of the publication of his pamphlet, he became an advisor to the duc d'Orléans.

But, given the state of the kingdom in the 1780s, the questions he was asking were pertinent:

> What is a nation? A body of associates living under common laws and represented by the same legislative assembly, etc. Is it not obvious that the nobility possesses privileges and exemptions which it brazenly calls its rights and which stand distinct from the rights of the great body of citizens? The Third Estate … contains everything that pertains to the nation while nobody outside the Third Estate can be considered as part of the nation. What is the Third Estate? Everything!

Here, Sieyès was meditating on a concept – nation – that was to become crucial in the early years of the revolution.

Decades on from Sieyès, Marxist historians would make their own judgements on the role of the Third Estate. But they used a different language. Whereas Sieyès (before the revolution) talked about 'rights' and 'fairness', those on the left (after the revolution) spoke of 'bourgeois revolution' and the 'development of class society'.

In fact, Marxist writers went further. With what should have been the benefit of hindsight, they tried to dovetail their left-wing theories with the historical evidence of the revolutionary period. Their interpretation of history was never going to be perfect – far from it; but, against all odds perhaps, they manufactured a view which became the orthodoxy. So, from the last decades of the nineteenth century through to the 1960s, the ideas of Lefebvre, Mathiez, Soboul and Jaurès reigned supreme.

In essence, these historians put forward a theory of 'overthrow'. Leaning heavily on the ideas of Marx, they argued that the French middle classes (the 'bourgeoisie') had shown themselves to be both successful and ambitious during the seventeenth and eighteenth centuries. But their aspirations for advancement – in political and economical terms – had been thwarted by the aristocracy, who were hanging on to power. They identified a growing tension between the bourgeoisie and aristocracy; and again in line with Marx, they argued that this conflict between capitalism and feudalism was inevitable – a necessary stage in the development of society (the final stage, of course, being communism).

In short, Marxists acknowledge the crisis that was afflicting the Old Regime and the feudal reaction of the aristocracy against the Crown; but they also go a step further and argue that the bourgeois class was not an innocent bystander but the *instrument* of political change; it took matters into its own hands and forcibly *overthrew* the system.

Thus, they argue that 1789 was a class revolution. The aristocracy had 'control' of the state but were usurped by the upwardly mobile middle class, or bourgeoisie, who, through the revolution, had gained the political power they required to supplement the economic power they had accumulated during the eighteenth century and before. For Marxists this was a historical law, an 'inevitable' scientific process – the bourgeoisie would *always* triumph over the aristocracy and capitalism would *always* overcome, and then replace, feudalism.

These Marxist ideas would gain ground, and become the orthodoxy, but they are open to attack on a number of fronts. First, the emphasis on class is questionable. No other factors were given much prominence – the actions of the King or the impact of the Enlightenment, for example. Marxists talked about classes as if they were totally homogenous and distinct, which of course they weren't. Shennan, for one, argues that in places the aristocracy and bourgeoisie almost merged: nobles invested in capitalist initiatives (giving rise to the term *notables*) and commercial and professional people owned land (hence the notion of 'bourgeois living nobly'). Second, the idea that feudalism gave way to capitalism was terribly simplistic. Society didn't work like that. There was some economic freedom before 1789 and, in reality, the revolution brought periods of regulation, state control and dictatorship as well as a general commitment to *laissez-faire* and capitalism. Likewise, the feudal system did not simply disappear. Remnants remained for decades, if not centuries, and it was naïve of the Marxist historians to believe that anything else could happen.

Finally, the 'overthrow' theory is very unclear about the nature of the revolution. Was there one revolution or several? Was it simply a 'bourgeois revolution' and nothing else? And if it was – as Marxists appear to claim – how do the people and peasants (and the aristocracy) fit in? These are significant questions and Marxist historians have not always had convincing answers. On the one hand, for obvious reasons, they have promoted a view of history which stresses the importance of 'collective mentalities', 'panics and plots' and the 'heroism of ordinary people'; but on the other, they are tied to the (slightly restricting) notion of 'bourgeois revolution', the idea that the revolution was one and indivisible and the product of the ambition of *one class alone*.

Marxists have tried to square the circle by arguing that the revolution of the bourgeoisie had 'knock-on effects' (the people and peasants becoming involved) but this is as good as admitting that the notion of 'bourgeois revolution' is a myth. Clearly, it is difficult to immunise the idea of a 'bourgeois' revolution from a general cross-class revolution – as Marxists have discovered to their cost.

The debate about origins and causation is complex and shows little sign of abating. We know that by the 1770s and 1780s the position of the monarchy was being questioned. The 'High' and 'Low' enlightenments had little in common except a growing mistrust of the political and religious establishment. What is more, the *cahiers* indicate that there was widespread frustration with the way that France was being governed. The situation was complicated by the political crisis of 1787–89 and the growing confidence of the middle classes.

There may be three broad perspectives on the issue, but there are scores of individual theories. It might almost be said that the narrative of the period has got lost amid the various theses and polemics.

3

The year of revolution: 1789

I owe it to myself. I owe it to my children, I owe it to my family and all my house to prevent the regal dignity which a long succession of centuries has confirmed in my dynasty from being degraded in my hands … I have chosen Your Majesty, as head of the second branch, to place in your hands this solemn protestation against my enforced sanction of all that has been done contrary to the royal authority since 15 July of this year and, at the same time, [my intention] to carry out the promises which I made by my declaration of the previous 25 June.

Louis XVI to Charles IV of Spain, 12 October 1789

Narrative overview: from the Estates General to the National Assembly

On 24 January 1789, for the first time since 1614, the Estates General was convoked. It met on 5 May, with voting taking place by estate rather than head. This was the central point of contention, with the Third Estate (who, as had in fact been agreed, were double the number of 1614) arguing that the practice of voting by estate should cease. On 28 May, the Third Estate started meeting on its own, and on 10 June, in opposition to the other two estates, it verified its own powers as the *communes* (commons). On 13 June, a number of priests elected to join with the Third Estate; and on 17 June, led by the Marquis de Mirabeau and the Abbé Sieyès, the Third Estate announced itself to be the National Assembly – a new body which incarnated the desires of the Third Estate, and also gave form to the idea of the nation as a voluntary and organic entity (on 9 July, it became the National Constituent Assembly).

The Third Estate declared, via the Tennis Court Oath on 20 June, that it would not cease its activities until a new constitution had been passed. Three days later the King held a Séance Royale and ignored the claims of the Third Estate to increased representation. But the day after, a group of clergy and nobles – including the Duke of Orléans – joined the Third Estate; and on 27 June, Louis was forced to recognise the National Assembly and instructed the First and Second estates to join the Third.

On 1 July, the King recruited extra troops to deal with the situation that was developing in the capital, and on 11 July, he sacked Necker as chief minister (but this was only announced to the people of Paris on the following day). On 14 July, the Bastille – a royal arsenal in the centre of Paris – was stormed during a popular insurrection. A group of mutinous members of the recently-formed National Guard, a new citizens' militia, also took part. Only seven prisoners were released (there were only this number of captives at the time), but amid the chaos, three significant people lost their lives: the governor of the Bastille, de Launay, the government minister, Foulon, and the Mayor of Paris, de Flesselles. On 15 July, Lafayette, an elected member of the Third Estate, became Commander of the National Guard, and on the next day Necker was recalled to government – a significant moment given his reputation as a reformer and a man of the people.

At the same time, the King began to pull his troops out of Paris, as if admitting that they were unreliable and he had lost the capital. On 18 July, Camille Desmoulins published a new newspaper, *La France libre*, which argued in favour of republicanism and, if necessary, violence. This indicated that the revolution was changing and evolving, as did the fact that, on 27 July, the King agreed to accept the tricolour cockade – symbolic perhaps of his growing acceptance of the revolution.

The focus of discontent switched to the countryside in late July. In many regions of France, peasants indicated their displeasure with the status quo by rioting and attacking key symbols of feudalism, including churches and chateaux. This came to be known as the 'Great Fear', and as a direct consequence, many aristocrats and priests opted to join the emigration. On the night of 4 August, the National Assembly adopted a set of measures which marked, at least on paper, the surrender of feudal rights (these became known as the August Decrees).

On 27 August, on the advice of the Marquis de Lafayette, the National Assembly adopted *The Declaration of the Rights of Man and of the Citizen* – in essence, the manifesto of France's new middle-class rulers. On 11 September, the King was granted a suspensive veto, which meant he could stall legislation, and he decided not to ratify the August Decrees (this did not happen until October). On 28 September, Jean Joseph Mounier was elected president of the National Constituent Assembly (which had evolved out of the National Assembly in July).

In October, there were mob riots in Paris and a group of poor women, upset by food shortages, marched on Versailles. This was a milestone in the course of the revolution. The monarchy was under pressure and the idea of constitutionalism, as opposed to absolutism, was gaining ground. Within days, Louis and the National Assembly had left Versailles for Paris – an important move that spoke of the monarch's desire, and need, to acknowledge the political change that was going on around him. However, the King also had a private face. On 12 October he wrote to his fellow monarch, Charles IV of Spain. It is clear from the passage cited at the beginning of the chapter that Louis was privately determined to maintain the power of the monarchy.

In this phase of the revolution, the key issue was the position of the King and the relationship between the King and the revolution. Would Louis be able to placate and also out-manoeuvre those who had grievances against the monarchy? Did he have the skill to negotiate a compromise between the different interest groups competing for power or the ability to assert his authority?

June: the Tennis Court Oath

The Tennis Court Oath was a landmark in the revolution. On 20 June 1789, members of the Third Estate found themselves locked out of their usual meeting place and, believing that the king was attempting to force them to disband, they convened in an indoor real tennis court near the Palace of Versailles where they vowed that they would continue to meet there until they had established a new constitution for France. Five hundred and seventy-six of them – plus a few members of other estates – signed the oath. The revolution was now in motion for, in effect, the Third Estate had declared itself to be the National Assembly. Their argument was that sovereignty and political authority now derived from this body rather than the King. Those present agreed that:

> … considering that it has been called to establish the constitution of the realm, to bring about the regeneration of public order, and to maintain the true principles of monarchy; nothing may prevent it from continuing its deliberations in any place it is forced to establish itself; and, finally, the National Assembly exists wherever its members are gathered. [And] Decrees that all members of this assembly immediately take a solemn oath never to separate, and to reassemble wherever circumstances require, until the constitution of the realm is established and fixed upon

solid foundations; and that said oath having been sworn, all members and each one individually confirm this unwavering resolution with his signature.

Jean Sylvain de Bailly, elected representative to the Estates General for Paris and president of the Third Estate, then rose and said: 'We swear never to separate ourselves from the National Assembly, and to reassemble wherever circumstances require, until the constitution of the realm is drawn up and fixed upon solid foundations.'

This was the moment when the Third Estate came together and agreed it would not disperse until it, as an estate, was given fairer representation within the French political system and a constitutional monarchy replaced the absolute monarchy. Vovelle calls it a 'revolution at the top'.

The oath had significant repercussions. On 23 June, the King published a thirty-five-point programme which confirmed the existence of the three individual estates – a move which alienated the Third Estate. The following day a group of clergy and nobles, including the Duke of Orléans, moved over to the Third Estate, and on 27 June, Louis officially recognised the National Assembly and suggested that the First and Second Estates join the Third.

On 11 July, Necker was dismissed. He had become unpopular in royal circles because he had been sympathetic to the calling of the Estates General and in favour of enhancing the representation of the Third Estate. Of course, when we say 'Third Estate' in this context, we mean the lawyers, merchants, doctors and financiers who were at the head of the Third Estate. They were envious of the Second Estate but also keen to cooperate with the nobles and the King in the regeneration of France; hence the Tennis Court Oath.

For their part, the King and Queen realised that in the aftermath of 20 June, conflict was on the horizon, and their fears were realised on 9 July when the National Constituent Assembly came into being – the embodiment of Third Estate aims and aspirations. Furthermore, there were tensions at the heart of government. While the King was generally sensitive to the political situation and conciliatory in his attitude – he saw himself as a paternalistic monarch, a benevolent father figure who listened and made genuine efforts to comprehend the demands of his people – the Queen was less so. As the wife of the King, she was close to the inner workings of the Court and was always going to be able to make her voice heard. But she was Austrian, slightly aloof, and had little feel for the concerns and aspirations of ordinary French people. At the same time, there was the question of Necker. Should his reforming ideas be taken on board or not?

According to Arthur Young, the Tennis Court Oath was the 'end' for the French monarchy. Historians have agreed with this verdict. Doyle argues that the revolution was now 'complete', while, from a Marxist perspective, Lefebvre says that almost on its own the oath 'effected the bourgeois revolution'.

July: the Fall of the Bastille

On 5 July 1789, Marshal de Broglie, leader of the royal army, announced,

> ... that with regard to the Bastille, there are two areas of concern: the commandant himself and the type of garrison. To obviate these difficulties I have advised His Majesty to instruct the Count de Puységur to confer with Monsieur de Villedeuil [Minister for the King's Household and Paris] and recommend a good senior officer who can be entrusted with commanding the Bastille. You must dispatch thirty Swiss Guards, today if you can but certainly tomorrow to augment the garrison ... Make

sure that they are under a very steady officer. As soon as the artillery regiment arrives, you must send in a small detachment of gunners to determine if the cannons are in good working order and to use them if it comes to that. This would be extremely unfortunate, but happily it is highly unlikely.

The Fall of the Bastille is probably the most famous moment of the entire revolution. The facts are these: the Bastille was a prison or arsenal, housing supplies of ammunition, and thus stood as a symbol of the autocratic methods of the Old Regime. On 14 July, as part of an insurrection, the people stormed the building and seven, perhaps eight, prisoners were released.

These bare details stand in contrast to the huge symbolism and mythology which has attached itself to the event. In short, the Fall of the Bastille is viewed as the moment when the revolution moved onto the 'streets'. Crucial here is the economic context. Paris had been affected by food shortages, unemployment, a rise in the price of basic foodstuffs and a public mood of dissatisfaction with levels of indirect taxation. A man named Keversau was one of those who charged the Bastille. His account may not be entirely reliable, but his allusion to the cross-class nature of the event is interesting: 'Veteran armies inured to war have never performed greater prodigies of valour than this leaderless multitude of persons belonging to every class, workmen of all trades who, mostly ill-equipped and unused to arms, boldly affronted the fire from the ramparts and seemed to mock the thunderbolts the enemy hurled at them.' He also explains how the episode ended:

In the intoxication of victory the unfortunate inmates of the dungeons of the Bastille had been forgotten. All the keys had been carried off in triumph and it was necessary to force the doors of the cells. Seven prisoners were found and brought to the Palais Royal. These poor fellows were in transports of

pleasure and could scarcely realise they were not the dupes of a
dream, soon to be dispelled. But soon they perceived the dripping
head of their tormentor stuck up on the point of a pike, above
which was a placard bearing the words: 'de Launay, Governor of
the Bastille, disloyal and treacherous enemy of the people.' At this
sight tears of joy flowed from their eyes and they raised their
hands to the skies to bless their first moments of liberty. The
keys were handed to M. Brissot de Warville, who, a few years
before, had been thrown into these caverns of despotism.

Thus, the urban masses had been mobilised and, essentially, the
Fall of the Bastille indicated that the King had lost his capital
city. On the significance of 14 July, Vovelle states that the
'popular revolution' had taken hold and the masses had emerged
during a process of political change. And for Doyle, the situation
was clear: royal authority had ceased.

Thereafter, discontent spread to most of the major towns and
cities in France, including Marseille, Strasbourg, Rouen and
Rennes. This was the 'Municipal Revolution', with royal
authorities reluctantly giving way to new ones. There were
other practical consequences and implications. For a start, the
King dispersed his troops. He was still displaying a protective
attitude towards the people, even after one of his advisors told
him: 'This is no revolt – this is revolution.' Bailly also felt the
need to intervene. In his memoirs he says:

It was decided to inform [the King] about what was worrying
the representatives and about the dangers posed to the people
and to himself. Consequently, the following decree was drafted:
'A delegation will be sent to the king to warn him of all the
dangers that threaten the capital and the kingdom and to show
him that the troops, whose mere presence is inflaming the
people's despair, need to be withdrawn.'

At the top of society, the Fall of the Bastille was viewed as a turning-point. Many royalists decided to emigrate rather than put themselves through the ignominy of seeing the King's authority totally diminished. They also feared for their lives. Led by the King's brother, the Comte d'Artois, they fanned out across Europe. They believed the royalist cause was temporarily lost in France but assumed that they would be returning soon.

Meanwhile, ordinary people were still aggrieved by the effects of inflation – Florin Aftalion says that corn and bread prices reached their highest ever level in July 1789 – and what they saw as the exploitative tendencies of local merchants. Of course, this was significant in itself, but, in theory at least, these two groups were now allies. The people of Paris had been responsible for the Bastille insurrection, while the merchants and the leaders of the Third Estate who spoke on their behalf made their voice heard through the Tennis Court Oath.

The involvement of the lower classes had brought with it the first suggestion of terror. On 14 July, the Governor of the Bastille had been hacked to death and his head paraded on a pike. This was a good three years before the onset of the Terror (most historians date it to September 1792) and as such did not bode well for the infant revolution. Indeed, as early as July, anyone displaying any kind of opposition to the revolution was vulnerable to attack, and this is why some historians have located the origins of the Terror in the summer of 1789.

At this point we should be cautious. Conservative historians tend to play down the significance of the Fall of the Bastille because there were only a handful of prisoners in the Bastille on 14 July. Surely, conservatives have claimed, this is testimony to the King's non-autocratic rule? Even Lefebvre, who in many ways idolises the ordinary people who effected the storming of the prison, says that, whatever its symbolic importance, 14 July did not 'settle' any issue.

In general terms, we can say that the Fall of the Bastille was a significant moment in the course of the revolution. On 16

July, Necker was recalled to office (after being sacked on 11 July) and the King's troops pulled out of Paris; on 18 July, the radical journalist Camille Desmoulins talked for the first time about the possibility of instituting a republic (although he remained in a tiny minority); and on 27 July, the King accepted the *tricolore* as the national flag.

August: the 'Great Fear'

In many ways, the revolution of the peasantry was the most original part of the revolution. French peasants were generally perceived to be either non-political or reactionary. Yet, in late July and early August, they took part in *La Grande Peur* (The Great Fear), attacking every symbol of feudalism they encountered, from castles to abbeys. The National Guard was involved in putting a stop to the rioting, but the violence seemed to intimidate the upper classes into countenancing concessions.

The night of 4 August has been viewed as the centre-point of the revolt. Peasants were nervous about the 1789 harvest and unsure about the intentions of their noble landlords. But it remained a spontaneous and disorganised rebellion, fuelled by a belief in an 'aristocratic plot'. It was not universal – many parts of France, including Brittany and Lorraine, remained untouched – and little thought had been given to the question of aims, objectives and what kind of regime, if any, the peasants might prefer.

So much had already happened in 1789 that the Great Fear was an almost inexplicable postscript. Was it momentum or did the peasants have a genuine political agenda? Whatever the truth, in what Doyle calls a 'moment of patriotic drunkenness', a member of the nobility proposed the abolition of feudalism. The resultant decree was passed on 11 August:

ARTICLE I. The National Assembly hereby completely abolishes the feudal system. It decrees that, among the existing rights and dues, both feudal and censuel, all those originating in or representing real or personal serfdom shall be abolished without indemnification. All other dues are declared redeemable, the terms and mode of redemption to be fixed by the National Assembly. Those of the said dues which are not extinguished by this decree shall continue to be collected until indemnification shall take place ...

VII. The sale of judicial and municipal offices shall be abolished forthwith. Justice shall be dispensed gratis. Nevertheless the magistrates at present holding such offices shall continue to exercise their functions and to receive their emoluments until the Assembly shall have made provision for indemnifying them ...

IX. Pecuniary privileges, personal or real, in the payment of taxes are abolished forever. Taxes shall be collected from all the citizens, and from all property, in the same manner and in the same form. Plans shall be considered by which the taxes shall be paid proportionally by all, even for the last six months of the current year.

But feudalism was not totally abolished. France was a huge country and feudal relationships were intrinsic to the way society was organised. Nevertheless, as an indicator of where the revolution was at, 4 August was a milestone.

The revolution of the peasantry had wide-ranging significance. First, it demonstrated that economic matters were still of paramount importance. The harvest of 1788 had been a failure – due to drought, snow and storms – and there were worries about 1789 too. The effect was a shortage of food and rising unemployment levels in rural areas. And by grabbing small parcels of land in the aftermath of 4 August, French peasants announced that they were no longer to be subservient in feudal terms. And second, the peasants' revolution had political ramifications. Would it be an asset or hindrance to the professional people at the top of the Third Estate? On one level, it had the potential to be the former. The two groups had the same enemies and, all things being equal, should have been able to work together. But on another level, it would almost certainly be the latter. Many business and professional people owned land and received feudal dues, and so they were a threat to the peasantry in the same way that the nobility was. And in broader terms, it was clear that the two classes had very different mentalities.

The *Declaration of the Rights of Man*

Later, on 26 August, the National Assembly approved the *Declaration of the Rights of Man*. The preamble read as follows: 'The representatives of the French people, organised as a National Assembly, believing that the ignorance, neglect, or contempt of the rights of man are the sole cause of public calamities and of the corruption of governments, have determined to set forth in a solemn declaration the natural, unalienable, and sacred rights of man.' This was a revolutionary statement. The idea of 'rights' rather than 'duties' echoed the work of Rousseau and Thomas Paine, the author of *The Rights of Man* and the idea of privilege was being questioned.

In its main body, the *Declaration* comprised 17 articles. Here there are some key indicators: the belief in equality is limited to rights; property is viewed as a right; and the 'nation' rather than an 'individual' (i.e. the King) is now sovereign. Thereafter, the document stressed a number of major themes including free speech, legality and freedom. So, the *Declaration* was revolutionary in many ways. But we should remind ourselves that at this

point the position of the King was not under threat. The 'constitutional articles', published as part of the *Declaration*, make this
plain. According to Article 2, 'The government of France is
monarchical: no authority in France is above the law by which
alone the King reigns and it is only in the name of the law that
he can require obedience.' And Article 3: 'The National
Assembly has recognised and declared as fundamental elements
in the French monarchy that the King's person is inviolable and
sacred; that the throne is indivisible and that the crown is hered-
itary.' Also, there were key omissions. The middle-class authors
had little to say about women, welfare or education. On 11
September, the National Assembly offered the King a suspensive
veto, which allowed him to stall legislation. Later in the same
month, Louis chose not to ratify the anti-feudalism decrees
passed by the National Assembly in August (only to change his
mind later). In October there was more protest. The Paris mob
revolted and the women of Paris began a symbolic march on
Versailles. Meanwhile, the royal palace was stormed and the
National Assembly moved to Paris.

Interpeting the revolution

Generally speaking, the revolution is best interpreted as a wave
of revolts that occurred in 1789, shaped successively by the
leaders of the Third Estate (June), ordinary people (July) and
peasants (August). But what kind of revolution was born? And
how should we interpret it? There are many different
approaches. Some historians conceive of it in geographical
terms. It was born in Paris and thereafter spread to the provinces
– the 'Municipal Revolution' – and had (sometimes unpredictable) reverberations in the countryside. Others see it through
the paradigm of class: an aristocratic revolution followed by
revolutions of the middle classes, the people and the peasantry.

The revolution can also be viewed in other ways. It was fundamentally political in the sense that at its core it was about representation and the competing claims of the First, Second and Third estates. At the same time it was a battleground, where concepts such as absolutism and liberalism took centre stage and had their adherents. By contrast, it was neither democratic nor socialist in orientation, though an embryonic egalitarianism did emerge, briefly, in 1793–94. Likewise, it could be argued that the revolution had important social and economic ramifications. As we have seen, according to the Marxist view – which held sway for much of the twentieth century – 1789 marked the triumph of the bourgeoisie and the demise of the landowning aristocracy.

We could also ask: was the revolution French or universal? The 'patriots' who emerged in the early 1790s certainly thought of it in nationalistic, and perhaps even chauvinistic, terms. But at the same time, there was a sense in which documents such as the *Declaration of the Rights of Man* were universal in design and potential application. That is why the Brissotins of 1792 wished to export the revolution to Europe and beyond. Another dichotomy is apparent too. A peaceable or violent revolution? At heart, of course, the revolutionaries preached love and fraternity, but relatively quickly the First Republic came to be associated with terror (at home) and war (across Europe).

4

The liberal revolution: 1790–92

By adopting the principles of the Constitution, and executing them in good faith, the People will come to learn the true cause of their misfortunes. Public opinion will change, since without it [my acceptance of the Constitution], only new convulsions could be expected … and I prefer to proceed towards a better order than that which would result from my refusal.

The King on the Constitution of 1791

Narrative overview: landmark declarations

In October 1789, Louis ratified the August Decrees (abolishing feudalism) and then moved to Paris with the National Assembly. The following month, all church property was nationalised and expropriated. In December, the *assignat* became legal tender; this was a new paper currency, originally conceived of as a bond secured against confiscated land. At the same time, the Assembly began to distinguish between 'active' (monied) and 'passive' (propertyless) citizens, with only the former being able to vote.

There were key developments in the early months of 1790: provinces replaced departments (January), all monastic vows and religious orders were suppressed (February), and – ironically, given what would follow in 1792 and later – the National Assembly renounced all involvement in wars of conquest (May).

Then, in landmark declarations, nobility was officially abolished (19 May) and priests were asked to swear an oath of loyalty to the state (12 July – the Civil Constitution of the Clergy).

Thereafter, we can detect the first tentative signs of the revolution becoming more radical. In August, the *parlements* were abolished; in September, Jacques Hébert's radical newspaper, *Le Père Duchesne*, was published for the first time; and in February 1791, Lafayette demanded the arrest of 400 armed aristocrats at the Tuileries.

Evident also is the self-interest of the middle classes, those who had come to power in 1789. On 2 March 1791, all trade guilds were abolished and on 14 June, legislation was passed banning trade unions – the Le Chapelier law. Also, the Jacobin Club, which had been established in 1789, split into moderates and radicals. The former – those who were proposing a constitutional monarchy and did not want to overthrow the King – came to be known as the Feuillants. The latter kept the name Jacobins. The split occurred in July 1791 following the publication of a controversial pamphlet by the Jacobin Club. The Feuillants would be labelled 'royalists', 'moderates' and 'aristocrats' by their enemies; but, for obvious reasons, there was little future for this political faction after the execution of the King.

Louis was uneasy with political developments. In public he had offered the revolution some lukewarm support but in private he was suspicious of the revolutionaries and their motives. Added to this, in April 1791 the National Guard stopped him from travelling to St. Cloud, Paris, to receive communion. The revolutionaries interpreted his proposed visit to St. Cloud as a blatant gesture in defiance of the revolution and one that might also herald some kind of 'escape' or 'plot' aimed at destabilising it. Meanwhile, the Queen was in regular communication with the Austrian royal family and hopeful of initiating some kind of rescue deal.

The issue came to a head in June when the royal couple and

members of their close family were arrested at Varennes while trying to flee the country via the north-eastern frontier. The escape plan had been poorly thought out: very few of the King's potential allies knew about it and his ultimate aim – of initiating some kind of counter-revolution from outside France – was vague. Louis and Marie-Antoinette had disguised themselves as Russian aristocrats but the King was recognised by a local postmaster. On 25 June, they were forced to return to Paris. But, even though they had been found out, and would henceforth be viewed with suspicion by many sections of the population, the National Assembly was in sympathetic mood: on 15 July, it declared the King to be inviolable and he was reinstated.

The Flight to Varennes had reverberations further afield. Across Europe, kings, queens, princes and dukes were unsure about how to respond. Of course, in their view, the revolution was an abomination and threatened the very concept of absolutism – a principle cherished by them all. But at the same time, *doing something* in support of the French monarchy would be dangerous and potentially counter-productive. In July 1791, Leopold II of Austria suggested a monarchical alliance in the Padua Circular, and in August, in the form of the Declaration of Pillnitz, the European powers settled for a statement of unity and outrage, which didn't hold them to any practical action.

On 14 September 1791, Louis XVI officially accepted the Constitution drawn up by the revolutionaries and a new Legislative Assembly was voted in. In the same month, the position of Jews in France was regularised:

> The National Assembly, considering that the conditions necessary to be a French citizen and to become an active citizen are fixed by the Constitution, and that every man meeting the said conditions, who swears the civic oath, and engages himself to fulfil all the duties that the Constitution imposes, has the right to all of the advantages that the Constitution assures.

This was a significant piece of legislation which suggested that, for all their narrow class objectives, the revolutionaries had a broader vision than some of their opponents might allege.

France had declared war on Austria in April 1792, so the European monarchs had to deal with the reality of military conflict rather than the possibility. In July, the Legislative Assembly announced that the 'fatherland was in danger' and Austria and Prussia issued the Brunswick Manifesto, which promised 'revenge' on the radical movement in France if members of the royal family were harmed (a sure sign, in the revolutionaries' eyes, that the King and Queen were in communication with the European monarchs). The two powers launched an invasion of France on 30 July.

At home, levels of patriotism were rising. In April, Rouget de Lisle published the *Battle Hymn of the Army of the Rhine*, which came to be known as the French national anthem, the *Marseillaise*. And in July, it was made compulsory for all males to wear the tricolour cockade. On 19 August, France was invaded by Coalition troops, and in September two of the most famous battles in French history took place: Verdun (a catastrophe at the hands of the Duke of Brunswick's troops) and Valmy (a huge triumph, with Coalition troops being halted in northern France). At this juncture, the convergence in thinking between the Brissotins (Girondins) and the Court should be noted. As Furet has argued, Brissot saw war as a vehicle for his own ambition, while Louis believed that it would enable him to make alliances that would ultimately lead to the revolution's collapse.

The politics of the situation were also changing. The Revolution of 10 August 1792 resulted in the suspension of the monarch and, in September, the dawn of the First French Republic. A new calendar was introduced, to mark the transition to a new type of society, and France entered Year 1 of a new and unpredictable era.

The Constitution of September 1791

What would follow on from the Tennis Court Oath, the Fall of the Bastille and the 'Great Fear'? Would there be more constitutional gains or a period of calm? Was it likely that the revolution would radicalise, turn back on itself, or even splinter? The liberal revolutionaries of 1789 had altered the political landscape and upset the fragile equilibrium of the nation. Was peace and consolidation a possibility? Here we will explore the period 1790–92, when the revolution was arguably at its most liberal. What were the key political events? And what values and ideas were dominant in these years?

The legacy of 1789 had been strong: a constitutional monarchy was on the verge of replacing an absolute one, the Third Estate had shown its growing strength, and a National Assembly had been established. What is more, the middle classes, people and peasants had articulated their grievances against 'the system'. No-one could claim that the relationship between the classes was harmonious – far from it – but it was obvious that a new France was emerging in embryonic form.

At this early juncture, the leaders of the revolution were moderate royalists. If we are looking for individuals who personify this phase, we should focus on Mirabeau and Lafayette. The Comte de Mirabeau was a writer and statesman who was in favour of France adopting a constitutional monarchy in the style of Great Britain. He was a noble but, following a rebuff from his fellow aristocrats, managed to get himself elected to the Estates General as a delegate of the Third Estate. This was indicative of Mirabeau: he had a clear understanding of the unfairness at the heart of the French political system and was sympathetic to the claims of the middle classes. Hence he was a key figure in the events leading up to, and following on from, the Tennis Court Oath; and he also engaged in secret negotiations with the monarchy in an attempt to bring the King and the revolutionaries closer. He died from heart problems on 2 April 1791.

The Marquis de la Fayette inhabited similar political space. He came from a large feudal family; however, on 19 June 1790, in an effort to show solidarity with the Third Estate, he renounced his nobility. Like Mirabeau, he favoured a constitutional monarchy; on 15 July 1789 he was appointed commander of the National Guard – the new militia of the revolution – and became a senior figure in the moderate political faction known as the Feuillants. He exited the political scene when the Jacobins came to power, but for a short period he and Mirabeau gave hope to those who wanted a peaceful, liberal and constitutional settlement.

The events of 1789 and the emergence of the Third Estate begged a significant question. How was France to be governed? There was general agreement that absolutism was now redundant and some form of constitutional monarchy was desirable.

The *Declaration of the Rights of Man*, published in late 1789, had laid down some general principles, but it was not a constitution. In many ways it was a 'holding operation'. It contained significant promises and, as such, gave the literate classes something to look to. At the same time, it also gave the revolutionaries a little time to think through what they wanted to do in terms of constitutional arrangements. The outcome was the Constitution of 3 September 1791. It set out with good intentions in its preamble: 'The National Assembly, wishing to establish the French Constitution upon the principles it has just recognised and declared, abolishes irrevocably the institutions which were injurious to liberty and equality of rights.' Many liberal themes were brought to life in this document: the hostility to feudalism and privilege, the belief in equality of opportunity, and also a lukewarm attitude to religion.

But probably the main point of interest – for contemporaries and later historians – was the King and what the Constitution said about his powers. On one level, the Constitution reiterated the point made in the *Declaration* of 1789: 'Sovereignty is one, indivisible, inalienable, and imprescriptible. It appertains to the nation; no section of the people nor any individual may assume the exercise thereof.' This seemed to sideline the King but in other articles he and his powers were referred to:

1. Monarchy is indivisible, and is delegated hereditarily to the reigning family, from male to male, by order of primogeniture, to the perpetual exclusion of women and their descendants …
2. The person of the King is inviolable and sacred; his only title is King of the French.
3. There is no authority in France superior to that of the law; the King reigns only thereby, and only in the name of the law may he exact obedience.

In effect, the Constitution of 1791 was creating a constitutional monarchy. A key role was assigned to the legislature:

1. The National Assembly constituting the legislative body is permanent and is composed of only one chamber.
2. It shall be formed every two years by new elections. Every period of two years shall constitute a legislature.
3. The provisions of the preceding article shall not apply to the next legislative body, the powers of which shall cease on the last day of April, 1793.
4. Renewal of the legislative body shall take place without need of sanction.
5. The legislative body may not be dissolved by the King.

The last point seemed to be the key one: the legislature and executive were now separate and the monarch could not interfere with the work of the National Assembly. The balance of power had been altered.

After a while, the constitution was officially accepted by the King. He wrote to his brothers, the Counts of Provence and Artois, with this news, and at the same time seemed to caution against further plotting against the revolution:

> You have no doubt been informed that I have accepted the Constitution and you are aware of the reasons that I gave to the Assembly ... The *émigrés* want nothing but revenge, and if they cannot make use of foreign arms, they will enter France alone, and will exact that revenge, even if they are all sure to die. War will thus be inevitable, because it is in the interest of those in authority. It will be horrible because it will be motivated by violence and despair. Can a king contemplate all these misfortunes with equanimity and bring them down upon his people? ... I have carefully weighed the matter and concluded that war presents no other advantages but horrors and more discord. I also believe then that this idea should be put aside and that I should try once again by using the sole means remaining to me, that of joining my will to the principles of the Constitution.

Clearly, the King was caught in a dilemma. As the Marquis de Bouille, a cousin of Lafayette, argued in his memoirs, 'Anyone who knew the King's religious character could not doubt that in taking his oath [to uphold the 1791 Constitution] his intention was to observe [it] scrupulously and execute the laws which it contained ... But this Constitution was then so imperfect; it was not finished; every day it became more vicious and impossible to uphold and implement.' The Constitution did little for other key players: the Queen called it 'monstrous' while radicals on the left argued passionately that it did not go far enough in transforming the political situation in France.

Two points should be emphasised at this juncture. First, France was in a state of flux. There was constant experimentation with the prevailing constitutional arrangements. By 1791 there was a charter of principles (the *Declaration*) and a first attempt at a constitution; on 1 October 1791, the Legislative Assembly replaced the National Assembly; and on 20 September 1792, the National Convention was established. This accompanied the birth of the First French Republic and followed pressure from the Paris Commune.

Second, in the period between 1789 and early 1792 there was a limit to the revolutionaries' ambitions. As we established earlier, there was no question of the revolution moving beyond moderate, liberal change. Or put another way: the democratic, republican cause had few, if any, adherents. Nobody had given a thought to abolishing the monarchy or executing the king. Of course, in time, and as attitudes to the monarchy hardened after the Flight to Varennes, this would change.

Potential threats – the Church and the monarchy

The property of the church was confiscated by the state on 2 November 1789. It was sold and, by way of compensation, each priest was paid 1,200 *livres* per year. The church monies were used to cover part of the public debt. A paper currency – the *assignat* – was also established, and this would be guaranteed against the confiscated church lands. In this sense, we can see how the sale of church lands had both economic and political effects.

Fear of counter-revolution – whether real or imagined – seemed to underpin the Civil Constitution of the Clergy, published by the revolutionaries on 12 July 1790. This was a detailed document laying down the status and duties of clergy under the revolution. Essentially, clergy were to swear an oath of loyalty to the regime – a strategy designed to create a schism between 'loyal' and 'rebel' priests. Articles XI and XXI of the Civil Constitution were crucial:

XI. Bishoprics and cures shall be looked upon as vacant until those elected to fill them shall have taken the oath …

XXI. Before the ceremony of consecration begins, the bishop elect shall take a solemn oath, in the presence of the municipal officers, of the people, and of the clergy, to guard with care the faithful of his diocese who are confided to him, to be loyal to the nation, the law, and the king, and to support with all his power the constitution decreed by the National Assembly and accepted by the king.

Elsewhere the document detailed how the Church would be organised, how bishops and priests would be elected, and how much they would be paid. Interestingly given the fact that France's new middle-class rulers were only lukewarm in their attachment to religion, one article announced that, 'The ministers of religion, performing as they do the first and most important functions of society and forced to live continuously in the place where they discharge the offices to which they have been called by the confidence of the people, shall be supported by the nation.' So, there was still an acknowledgement that the Church was an important part of French society; but, at the same time, the legislation turned parish priests into civil servants almost overnight. The oath was a significant development, and historians still regard it as such. Doyle calls it a key turning-point in the course of the revolution, while Bosher says that it divided the nation more than any other measure. This, of course, was the intention.

If Catholic priests were a potentially destabilising force, so was the monarchy. In the early years of the revolution, Louis was able to maintain his position at the summit of the French political system. But it was a precarious one. Of course, as Vovelle notes, hardly anyone had thought of doing without him. He was a father figure and still generally loved; instead, it was the regime and the system that was attracting criticism.

Moreover, he was happy to go along with the changes made in and after 1789, at least in public.

But, towards the end of 1790, Louis started to reveal his hand. On 20 November, he wrote to Monsieur le Baron de Breteuil, his former foreign minister. The letter reveals the extent of the King's disenchantment:

> Since circumstances do not permit me to give you my instruc-
> tions on such and such a matter and to have a continuous corre-
> spondence with you, I am sending you this present to serve as
> plenipotential powers and authorisation vis-a-vis the various
> powers with whom you may have to treat on my behalf. You
> know my intentions and I leave it to your discretion to make
> such use of it as you think necessary for the good of my service.
> I approve of everything that you do to achieve my aim, which
> is the restoration of my legitimate authority and the happiness
> of my peoples. Upon which, Monsieur le Baron, I pray God
> that he keep you in His holy protection.

The coded talk of 'instructions' and 'intentions' suggested that the King was about to make some kind of move. The memoirs of the Marquis de Bouille also shed interesting light on the King's position. They tell of a man who was both unhappy and frustrated and who would only resort to force in the last instance. Bouille writes:

> The King, who had read a lot of history and during the
> Revolution preferred to read that of England, had remarked
> that James II had lost his throne because he left his kingdom and
> that Charles I's death sentence had been grounded on the fact
> that he had levied war on his subjects; these reflections, which
> he often communicated to me, instilled in him an extreme
> repugnance to leaving France to put himself at the head of his
> troops or to cause them to move against his revolted peoples.

The defining moment for the King was the Flight to Varennes in June 1791. Among historians the consensus view is that after Varennes the King lost his credibility and 'died' in the eyes of his subjects. Historians have argued that this was a turning-point: constitutional monarchists lost heart and started to conceive of a France without a monarch.

Within fourteen months the monarchy had been abolished. On 10 August 1792, 20,000 people stormed the Tuileries in what Robespierre called the 'most gorgeous revolution'. The revolutionary authorities suspended the King and by September France had formally become a republic with a new National Convention replacing the old Legislative Assembly.

Radical clubs and societies

Many new political organisations were formed in the period following the revolutionary events of 1789. On the right, Club des Valois, Club des Impartiaux, Club Monarchique and others spread royalist propaganda. And on the left, scores of revolutionary clubs and societies were established to promote the revolutionary cause. Cobban estimates that there were between 5,000 and 8,000 such organisations by 1793 with a total membership of almost half a million. Radical and intellectual in nature, they were akin to debating societies or pressure groups and in Paris they gradually became an alternative centre of power. They took various jobs upon themselves, such as organising festivals, distributing reading material and encouraging all kinds of pro-revolutionary activity.

There were many revolutionary clubs, including the Club of '89 and Society of Friends of the Rights of Man and of the Citizen or Cordeliers Club, but the biggest was the Jacobin Club. As early as 1790 it had around 150 affiliated branches. In his diary, Arthur Young, the English writer, described a typical meeting:

> There were above one hundred deputies present, with a president in the chair; I was handed to him, and announced as the author of the *Arithmetique Politique* … In this club the business that is to be brought into the National Assembly is regularly debated; the motions are read that are intended to be made there, and rejected or corrected and approved. When these have been fully agreed to, the whole party are engaged to support them.

What is impressive here is the level of attendance and the business-like manner in which the meeting was conducted.

In political terms, the clubs were in favour of reform. They harried and harangued the authorities, always wanting to take the revolution in a more radical direction. In time they would become absolutely fundamental to the revolution, taking on practical tasks previously undertaken by the municipal authorities and also supplying the revolution with some of its most brilliant leaders.

But clearly, in the early years of the revolution, the major issue was the King. Jacobin Club members were wary of Louis; and suspicion turned to mistrust after Varennes. In protest at his actions, they drew up a petition against the monarch. Its last lines read:

> Considering, finally, that it would be as contrary to the majesty of the outraged nation as to its interests to entrust the reins of the empire to a perfidious, traitorous fugitive; Formally and expressly demands that the National Assembly accept, in the nation's name, Louis XVI's abdication on 21 June of the crown delegated to him, and provide for his replacement by all constitutional means. The undersigned declare that they will never recognise Louis XVI as their king, unless the majority of the nation expresses a desire contrary to that contained in the present nation.

It should be noted that as late as 16 July 1791 – the date the petition was published – the Jacobin Club was talking in terms of 'constitutional means'; but this was soon to change.

5

War and terror: 1792–94

Every day we learn of new betrayals and new crimes. Every day we become upset at the discovery and the reappearance of new conspiracies.

Terror is the Order of the Day, 5 September 1793

Narrative overview: the ascendancy of the Jacobins

In this period we see the emergence of two main revolutionary groupings: Girondins and Jacobins. This was an indication that the revolution was already haemorrhaging. No longer was there simply one revolutionary party, but rather two main factions, two different sets of people and, more importantly, two contrasting views about the aims of the revolution.

Both Girondins and Jacobins would have described themselves as passionate revolutionaries but they were fundamentally different in their outlook. Whereas the former were happy with 1789 and wanted to protect the gains of that year, the latter saw it merely as a starting-point. The Girondins were moderate by instinct, the Jacobins radical. In time, where members of the factions sat in the National Assembly would come to designate two new approaches to politics: the Girondins sat on the right, the Jacobins on the left.

The major sticking point was war. And here perhaps the

differing standpoints were the opposite of what one might have predicted. The Girondins were evangelistic: they wanted to take the battle to Europe, spread the ideas of the revolution, and also use war as a means of 'flushing out' the King and potential enemies. The Jacobins, by contrast, were more reserved. They – Robespierre in particular – felt that France had a lot to lose by involving herself in an unpredictable war, and so argued that consolidation at home rather than aggression abroad was the best policy.

The rivalry between the factions could be witnessed inside and outside the National Assembly, but it was not the only major tension afflicting France at this time. There were conflicts of interest involving the peasants, townspeople and middle classes; rivalries between officials in the provinces and the capital; and men of the revolution were increasingly concerned by the growing threat of the counter-revolution.

The Storming of the Tuileries Palace on 10 August 1792 marked the fall of the monarchy. It could be argued that the Terror began in September 1792 with the September Massacres. In their wake came a number of momentous events: the epic military success at Valmy (20 September), the meeting of the Convention (21 September) and the abolition of royalty (21 September). The new revolutionary calendar – introduced in 1793 – took 22 September 1792 to be the birth date of the First French Republic.

In the foreign-policy sphere, this period also witnessed France's occupation of Nice and Savoy, the French victory at Jemappes and the occupation of Belgium. On 15 December, a decree was passed detailing how the new 'occupied territories' should be treated. In early 1793, France declared war on Great Britain and Spain.

During December 1792, the Convention reconstituted itself as a tribunal and put the King on trial. He was executed on 21 January 1793. In the months that followed, the infrastructure of the Terror was established. The Revolutionary Tribunal, an Inquisition-style court, was set up in March and the Committee of Public Safety, the key executive body of the period, started work on 6 April. In May, the Committee of General Security was formed to oversee police work and the first law of the Maximum, initiating a price ceiling, was also published. But still there was something of an institutional hiatus.

Maximilien Robespierre became the central personality of the period. He was born in Arras and followed his father into the legal profession. He was elected to the Estates General in May 1789 and later sat in the National Constituent Assembly and National Convention. During this period he gained a reputation as a charismatic orator and a fierce opponent of the monarchy. In April 1790, he was elected president of the radical Jacobin Club and campaigned for the establishment of a republic and the execution of the King. A year later, in May 1791, Robespierre was responsible for the motion which said that deputies who sat in the Constituent Assembly could not sit in the legislature which succeeded it. He would come to be known as 'The Incorruptible'.

As the revolution shifted leftwards after 1792, Robespierre became an increasingly significant figure. Throughout 1793, his political dominance over the Brissotins/Girondins was consolidated. The conflict was played out in the Jacobin Club and on the streets of Paris. Between 31 May and 2 June 1793 there were demonstrations outside the Convention – the end result being that the Girondin faction was neutralised, if not eliminated. This Jacobin 'coup' heralded the voting of the Constitution of 1793 on 24 June. Though this document was stillborn – it was never instituted due to the onset of 'revolutionary government' in October 1793 – it stood as a key marker of the trajectory of the revolution. In July, the radical Jean-Paul Marat was assassinated, Robespierre entered the Committee of Public Safety and all remaining seigneurial rights were abolished without compensation.

Key legislation followed. In August, the *levée en masse* brought mass conscription; later, on 5 September, the Convention, under the influence of the people of Paris, acted to formalise what came to be known popularly as the 'Reign of Terror'. On 17 September, the all-embracing Law on Suspects was published, and on 29 September, the General Maximum – introducing across-the-board price ceilings, thus helping ordinary consumers - was passed. In October, the policy of Dechristianisation was unveiled; this was an attack on Catholicism and the influence of the Catholic Church. In the same month, Marie-Antoinette and leading Girondins were executed. On 4 December 1793, the Law of Revolutionary Government was passed, which led to the centralisation of power in the Committee of Public Safety.

Robespierre's dominance was unquestionable, not simply in terms of political repression, but also in terms of the war effort (his initial reservations had been overtaken by events) and the shape that the religious and economic terrors would take. In theory, all members of the Committee of Public Safety were equals, but there was no denying the fact that in time Robespierre became its de facto leader.

The execution of the King

On 11 December 1792, the King of France was indicted by the revolutionaries: 'Louis, the French people accuse you of having committed a multitude of crimes in order to establish your tyranny by destroying its liberty.' There followed a list of thirty-three crimes the King had allegedly committed. From no.1, 'On 20 June, 1789, you attacked the sovereignty of the people by suspending the assemblies of its representatives and by driving them by violence from the place of their sessions', to no.33, 'You caused the blood of Frenchmen to flow.'

Louis' demise was now inevitable. On 23 January 1793 his execution was proclaimed:

> Citizens, the tyrant is no more. For a long time the cries of the victims, whom war and domestic dissensions have spread over France and Europe, loudly protested his existence. He has paid his penalty, and only acclamations for the Republic and for liberty have been heard from the people ... Now, above all, we need peace in the interior of the Republic and the most active surveillance of the domestic enemies of liberty. Never did circumstances more urgently require of all citizens the sacrifice of their passions and their personal opinions concerning the act of national justice which has just been effected. Today the French people can have no other passion than that for liberty.

The final word in this statement is worth dwelling on. *Liberté*. It was a key outcome of 1789, a cherished achievement. But in the period between 1792 and 1794, the word lost its meaning. The revolutionaries started to use the word too often, in too many contexts. The execution of the King; the introduction of the Terror; the declaration of war. In reality, would all these events add to the sum total of liberty? Or were the revolutionaries simply deluding themselves?

By April 1792, France was at war with Austria, and by autumn of the same year, it is argued, the Terror had begun in earnest with the September Massacres when more than 1,000 prisoners were murdered, allegedly on the instructions of Danton (who had played a key role in the overthrow of the monarchy and would become the first president of the Committee of Public Safety). As such, from the autumn of 1792, the revolution was simultaneously at its most expansive and radical. For the moderate, liberal revolution, this was the beginning of the end. Here we will explore the topics of war and revolutionary terror. First, we will assess the debate within the revolutionary camp about the merits of making war on Europe. Then we will briefly consider the course of the war. Moving on, we will examine the nature of the Terror before discussing its origins: was it planned and an intrinsic part of the revolutionaries' ideology or merely the product of circumstance?

Revolutionary war: 'the bloody flag is raised'

The debate about war revealed an interesting and important schism within the revolution. By way of background, it should be pointed out that many of the revolutionaries' initial goals had been achieved in the period following the Tennis Court Oath, the Fall of the Bastille and the Great Fear. The moderate, liberal revolution had triumphed and the achievements were many: equality before the law, the end of feudalism, the rights of man, a constitutional monarchy and then a republic. However, it could be argued that by 1792 there was a void developing. There had been achievements, and the King and Queen had played into the revolutionaries' hands by revealing an attitude that was part ambiguous about the revolution and part hostile. But what next? Where did the revolution go from here?

This was the question on which the revolutionaries split into one very large faction and one very small one. The Girondins – or Brissotins, as they were also known on account of their leader, Jacques-Pierre Brissot – wanted to take the revolution forwards. In their view, this meant taking the revolution abroad, exporting it to Europe and perhaps beyond. In a speech to the National Assembly, Brissot stated: 'France wants peace but does not fear war ... War is necessary to France for her honour, external security, internal tranquillity, to restore our finances and public credit, to put an end to terror, treason and anarchy ... This war is a public benefit.' Twenty-four hours later he announced: 'Either we will win and restore public credit and our prosperity or we will be beaten and the traitors will finally be convicted and punished. I have only one fear; it is that we won't be betrayed. We need great treasons, our salvation lies there, because there are still strong doses of poison in France and strong emetics are needed to expel them.'

The language was almost evangelical: France had wonderful news that she wanted to share with the wider world. 'Liberty, equality, fraternity': these were the radical ideas that she wished to promote. In the view of the Brissotins, war would have many benefits and advantages, both economic and political. It has to be said that most of the revolutionaries were persuaded by the arguments of Brissot. And that the faction which started to openly oppose Brissot was only tiny.

For Robespierre, the leader of the Jacobins, things were less clear-cut: 'It seems to me those who desired to provoke war adopted this view only because they did not pay sufficient attention to the nature of the war that we shall undertake and to the circumstances in which we today find ourselves.' In summary, he felt that war would be dangerous and unpredictable and was concerned about committing France to a path that could prove counter-productive. As we know, France went to war and became embroiled in conflict for a generation. But it is interesting to note the forces that were ranged against each other in the debate about war. Brissot, the moderate Girondin, was pushing for war, while Robespierre, the radical Jacobin, was against. Then there was the King. He was, at the same time, a bystander and key player in the unfolding situation. He was still titular head of government and thus, even though the revolutionaries were making and dictating policy, protocol dictated that he should sign the official declaration of war against Austria in April 1792. In a sense, this was a bizarre state of affairs but Louis had plenty to gain from the revolutionaries' commitment to war. If the military conflict went well, the possibility existed that the

King, as the man who took France into war, would be cemented in power and able to play on the fact that 'his' war had been a triumph. If this happened, he might be left with the opportunity to restore order at home. On the other hand, if the war was a failure, the King could hope that the revolution – which had staked so much on its 'war against despots' – might crumble and disintegrate. And if this happened, the monarchs of Europe might be inclined to intervene and ensure the restoration of Bourbon authority.

On 20 April 1792, France formally declared war against Austria. Four days later, Claude-Joseph Rouget de Lisle, a captain in the engineers and an amateur Strasbourg-based musician, devised the rousing patriotic song that would become the soundtrack to the French military effort in 1792 and, eventually (in 1795), the national anthem of France.

> Let us go, children of the fatherland,
> Our day of Glory has arrived.
> Against us stands tyranny,
> The bloody flag is raised,
> The bloody flag is raised.
> Do you hear in the countryside
> The roar of these savage soldiers?
> They come right into our arms
> To cut the throats of your sons, your country.
> To arms, citizens!
> Form up your battalions.
> Let us march, Let us march!
> That their impure blood
> Should water our fields.

On 28 April 1792, France invaded the Austrian Netherlands and by 5 July, the Legislative Assembly had announced that the 'fatherland' was in danger.

There were two major developments at the end of July. On 25 July, the Duke of Brunswick, commander of the Austrian and Prussian armies, issued the Brunswick Manifesto. The document was addressed to the people of France:

> Convinced that the sane portion of the French nation abhors the excesses of the faction which dominates it, and that the majority of the people look forward with impatience to the time when they may declare themselves openly against the odious enterprises of their oppressors, his Majesty the emperor and his Majesty the King of Prussia call upon them and invite them to return without delay to the path of reason, justice, order, and peace.

The aim was to divide and rule – to speak to the 'sensible' part of the population in the hope that they may disown the leaders of the revolution in Paris. An offer was also made: if the King's safety was guaranteed, the foreign powers would behave with circumspection. And on 30 July, Austria and Prussia invaded France. Predictably, by August the revolution was on the back foot. Lafayette had fled to Austria and coalition troops, led by the Duke of Brunswick, had triumphed at Verdun. But there was respite at Valmy on 20 September when the Coalition forces were halted.

Sixteen months into the war – on 23 August 1793 – the revolutionary authorities introduced the *levée en masse*. This was conscription on a massive scale, with 800,000 young Frenchmen forcibly called up to military service:

1. From this moment until that in which the enemy shall have been driven from the soil of the Republic, all Frenchmen are in permanent requisition for the service of the armies. The young men shall go to battle; the married men shall forge arms and transport provisions; the women shall make

      tents and clothing and shall serve in the hospitals; the children shall turn old linen into lint; the aged shall betake themselves to the public places in order to arouse the courage of the warriors and preach the hatred of kings and the unity of the Republic.

2. The national buildings shall be converted into barracks, the public places into workshops for arms …

Further, Article 7 announced that no-one could evade the draft. France was entering a period of strict dictatorial government.

What does all this say about the revolution? First, that there was now a momentum to events; the revolutionaries had achieved as much as they could at home and were now looking further afield. Second, that patriotism had become a major issue; either you were 'with' the revolution, and believed in the war, or you didn't and you were automatically a 'suspect'. And third, that the foreign powers had failed to live up to expectations. They had issued the Declaration of Pillnitz, agreeing to 'use the most efficient means in relation to their strengths to place the King of France in a position to be totally free to consolidate the bases of a monarchical government' and 'to act quickly, in mutual agreement, and with the forces necessary to achieve the proposed and common goal', but it is generally agreed that their efforts were half-hearted and ultimately unsuccessful.

The Terror: dispensing 'revolutionary justice'

Between 31 May and 2 June 1793, the Mountain (the Jacobins) outmanoeuvred the Plain (the Girondins). Louis-Marie Prudhomme, founder of the radical newspaper *Révolutions de Paris*, describes the scene:

At three o'clock on Friday morning, 31 May, the alarm
sounded in several parts of the city and quickly spread to all the
others … If the mood wasn't uniform, the concert of wills
proved to be perfect. Everyone ran to their post, meaning to
their sections. However, in several streets, the means that we
have already mentioned were being used. The citizens stood
guard in front of their doors. At eight o'clock there were more
than 100,000 men under arms, united, brothers, all determined
to perish before letting the national legislature be threatened.

This was the coup that radicalised the revolution.

On 24 June 1793, the revolutionaries issued their second
constitution. It was never formally adopted, but it stood as a
marker of the trajectory of the revolution. Many of its articles
and phrases were reminiscent of those contained in the
Declaration of 1789 and the Constitution of 1791, but at the same
time it pushed the revolution in a radical direction:

1. The aim of society is the public good …
18. Every man may engage his services and his time but he
    may neither sell himself nor be sold. He does not have an
    alienable property in himself. The law does not recognise
    domestic service: all that can exist is a contract for the
    payment of services rendered between the man who
    works and the man who employs him …
21. Public assistance is a sacred debt. Society owes a living to
    unfortunate citizens either by providing them with work
    or by giving those unable to work the means of subsis-
    tence.

The tone is left-wing: the hostility to slavery, the emphasis on
welfarism and egalitarianism, and the belief that 'society' was
more important than the 'individual'. But there were also
warning signs. Take, for example, the final article, 124, which

said that 'The Declaration of Rights and the Constitutional Act shall be engraved on tablets within the legislative body and in public places.' Was this a harmless exercise in public information or a step on the road to state propaganda?

In 1794, Robespierre put forward a personal vision:

> In our country, we want to replace egoism with morality, honour with honesty, the tyranny of fashion with the rule of reason, contempt for misfortune with contempt for vice, insolence with self-respect, vanity with greatness of soul, love of money with love of *gloire*, good company with good people, intrigue with merit, wit with genius, show with truth, the tediousness of dissipation with uncloyed happiness, the pettiness of *les grands* with the greatness of man, an amiable, frivolous and wretched people with one that is magnanimous, strong and happy, that is to say all the vices and stupidities of the monarchy with all the virtues and miracles of the Republic (applause).

These were fine sentiments – Robespierre talked about a 'Republic of Virtue' – but what did they mean? Did the practice match the theory?

Between 1792 and 1794 there were approximately 40,000 victims of the Terror. In his work, Fife has depicted the era of the Terror as one of sinister politicking and psychotic excesses, while Arasse has traced the evolution of the guillotine from 'humane instrument of justice' to 'sword of liberty', arguing that 'Just as the revolutionary government was the incarnation of the will of the people it represented, so the guillotine gave form to revolutionary law: the people had an instrument that fittingly represented it in the execution of its justice.' In this sense, the guillotine was symbolic of how the noble aims of the early revolution had been lost in anarchy and chaos.

The September Massacres of 1792 were, arguably, the first sign of organised state violence. Over 1,200 prisoners were killed in a period of sporadic mob violence, with followers of Brissotin and Robespierre blaming each other for the deaths. A year later, on 5 September 1793, the Convention declared that the Terror was both inevitable and desirable:

> Every day new disturbances stir up the Republic, ready to drag it into their stormy whirlwinds, hurling it into the bottomless abyss of the centuries to come ... Where is that powerful being who will crush all these reptiles who corrupt everything they touch and whose venomous stings stir up our citizens, transforming political gatherings into gladiatorial arenas where each passion, each interest, finds apologists and armies? Legislators, it is time to put an end to the impious struggle that has been going on since 1789 between the sons and daughters of the nation and those who have abandoned it. Your fate, and ours, is tied to the unvarying establishment of the republic. We must either destroy its enemies, or they will destroy us.

It is not advisable to talk of the Terror in the singular. Many commentators and historians do, but where possible it is much more helpful to speak of it in the plural. There were, it is generally agreed, three main arms to the Terror: political, economic and religious. While the political terror is best known, on account of its overarching nature and the blood-letting that accompanied it, it is the economic and religious terrors that arguably tell us more about the nature of the revolution in the period 1793–94.

The political terror was centred on legal and judicial structures: the Committee of General Security, which focused on intelligence-gathering, policing and surveillance; the Revolutionary Tribunal, a kind of 'Inquisition' body that dispensed 'revolutionary justice'; representatives on mission, who enforced the will of Paris in the provinces; revolutionary committees, which monitored residents in every municipality;

and the various revolutionary armies that roamed the country-side with orders to clamp down on federalist and counter-revolutionary activity (in terms of definition, federalists wanted independence from Paris, while counter-revolutionaries demanded a return to the old monarchical regime). Overseeing everything was the Committee of Public Safety – the chief executive organ.

A key piece of legislation – the Law of Suspects – was passed on 17 September 1793. This was a catch-all decree which served to highlight the atmosphere of paranoia that was now affecting France. Its first two articles read as follows:

1. Immediately after the publication of the present decree, all suspected persons within the territory of the Republic and still at liberty shall be placed in custody.

2. The following are deemed suspected persons: 1st, those who, by their conduct, associations, talk, or writings have shown themselves partisans of tyranny or federalism and enemies of liberty; 2nd, those who are unable to justify, in the manner prescribed by the decree of 21 March last, their means of existence and the performance of their civic duties; 3rd, those to whom certificates of patriotism have been refused.

Everyone, it seemed, was a potential suspect. The decree also went on to talk about 'watch committees'.

In essence, the economic terror meant a planned economy, with the state taking on all aspects of distribution and exchange. A price 'maximum' was introduced to assist consumers (the revolution had to have these people on its side) and, as if to highlight the gravity of the wartime situation, all hoarders would henceforth be executed. The Ventôse Decrees were the centre-piece of the economic terror. They were read out to the Convention by St. Just, a member of the Committee of Public Safety, on 3 March 1794:

1. All the Communes of the Republic will draw up a list of needy patriots including their names, ages, occupations and the numbers and ages of their children. The district authorities will send their lists to the Committee of Public Safety as soon as possible.
2. When the Committee of Public Safety has received these lists it will draw up a report on means of indemnifying all the destitute with the property of the enemies of the Revolution on the basis of a schedule provided by the Committee of General Security which will also be published.

The talk of 'needy patriots' and 'the destitute' emphasised the government's new 'welfarist' agenda, while the mention of 'surveillance committees' suggested a creeping totalitarianism once more.

The religious terror was similar to the economic terror in its ideological nature. If the Ventôse Decrees were aiming to create a new kind of society – egalitarian and levelling – the statements emanating from the revolutionary dictatorship on religion suggested that it had grandiose and over-ambitious dreams in the cultural realm.

There were two main strands to the religious terror. One was atheism – a war on Catholicism that came to be known as 'Dechristianisation'. This involved the destruction of churches and religious monuments and was supported by the Hébertists, followers of the radical journalist Jacques Hébert. It also heralded a new republican calendar. This was a major step and, more than anything else perhaps, illustrated the delusional nature of the revolutionary regime. It was announced that: 'The era of the French begins with the foundation of the Republic, which took place on 22 September 1792 of the common era, the day the sun reached the true autumnal equinox, entering the sign of Libra at nine o'clock, eighteen minutes, thirty seconds in the morning, as measured by the Paris Observatory.' Officials were also interested in practicalities: 'The Committee on Public Instruction is charged with having the calendar printed in various formats, with a simple explanation of its principles and most frequent uses.' It must have seemed like an ambitious enterprise. But that did not stop officials of the revolution trying to justify it. Fabre d'Eglantine, who served on the commission that drew up the calendar, argued thus: 'We could no longer count the years during which kings oppressed us as an era during which we had lived. The prejudices of the throne and the church, and the lies of each, sullied each page of the calendar we were using.' Also instituted were a range of new revolutionary cults including the Cult of Reason.

The other strand was associated with Robespierre. He wanted to move beyond atheism. He understood the power of religion and the extent to which ordinary people were attached to the idea of believing in something. So he did not dispense with religion altogether – he simply invented a new creed which (he hoped) the same people would come to embrace. He put forward the idea of a non-Christian deity: the Supreme Being.

On 7 May 1794, a decree announced the birth of a new state religion:

> The French people recognises the existence of the Supreme Being and the immortality of the soul ... It recognises that the proper worship of the Supreme Being consists in fulfilling ... duties ... It places in the forefront of these duties: to abominate bad faith and tyranny, to punish tyrants and traitors, to succour the needy, to respect the weak, to defend the oppressed, to do to others all the good that is in our power and to be unjust to no one.

And implicit in the new religion were a batch of new festivals: 'They will take their names from the glorious events of our

Revolution, from the virtues dearest to man and most useful to him and from the greatest benefits of nature … Every year the French Republic will celebrate the festivals of 14 July 1789, 10 August 1792, 21 January 1793 and 31 May 1793.'

Significantly, freedom of worship was not allowed for – contradicting one of the earlier promises of the revolution.

The Terror and war

For historians the main debate about the Terror relates to origins and causation. Was it planned and premeditated or was it the product of pragmatism and circumstance? Or was it an event/period that actually defies logical analysis? Those on the right or hostile to the revolution would suggest that the Jacobins had an ideological vision of where they wanted to take the revolution. They had conspired to establish an egalitarian society and a new kind of religion; and a 'single will' was a necessity. This argument implies that the Terror was programmed and planned; it was dogmatic, ideological and also anathema to the values of the early 'liberal' revolution.

But, events were playing their part. It is characteristic of apologetic lines of argument to point out that the reality of war and the beginnings of counter-revolution encouraged the Jacobins into dictatorship and intolerance. At the same time, the Robespierre regime was being lobbied by the *sans-culottes* – ordinary urban folk who had been instrumental in the overthrow of the monarchy and thereafter alternated between supporting and making life uncomfortable for the Jacobin regime – and the *enragés*, led by Jacques Roux, who wanted economic rather than abstract political rights. The emergence of both groups illustrated the radicalisation of the revolution.

How should we summarise the relationship between war and terror? In many ways they were opposite sides of the same coin:

state-sponsored violence abroad and at home. As policies they were instituted at approximately the same time and predicated on similar sentiments – most notably, patriotism and the need for security in the face of 'counter-revolutionary' threats. What is more, as Mona Ozouf has shown, there was often a symbiotic relationship between revolutionary war and terror: they inspired each other.

While all this was happening, the counter-revolutionary coalition was taking shape.

6

The Counter Revolution

I therefore propose to you, as I propose to the Kings of Spain, England, Prussia, Naples, and Sardinia, as well as to the Empress of Russia, to unite with them and me to consult on cooperation and measures to restore the liberty and honour of the Most Christian King and his family, and to limit the dangerous extremes of the French Revolution.

The Padua Circular, 5 July 1791

Narrative overview: reacting to the revolution

The consensus among historians is that the Counter Revolution had enormous potential but achieved very little. At root, it was an instinct and impulse. The events of 1789 had startled and provoked many. The question was how to react to the revolution. Some took up arms and organised resistance; others articulated their hostility in writing, in philosophical treatises. Either way, the revolution was a point of departure, a moment in time when political choices became stark.

Here we must remind ourselves that in 1789, in the National Assembly, the terms 'left' and 'right' had been born. In time, through the 1790s and beyond, these positions hardened. The Counter Revolution can be seen as the epitome, and most extreme form, of right-wing politics in this period. In his writings, Godechot talks about the 'doctrine' and 'action' of the Counter Revolution, as if they were distinct. Likewise, Roberts implies there was a Counter Revolution of the 'interior' and 'exterior'. It is interesting to note these views at the outset.

There is a direct relationship between the revolution and the Counter Revolution. The emigration began as soon as the Bastille fell. Thereafter, every significant milestone in the revolution encouraged more aristocrats and priests – and dislocated members of the Third Estate – to leave France. There were around 150,000 émigrés in total, including Louis' two brothers, Comte d'Artois and Comte de Provence. Coblenz in the Rhineland served as their headquarters but, although they promised much, the émigrés did not impress the various European courts. The irony, however, was that the revolutionaries in Paris took them extremely seriously and passed a number of laws against them.

At the same time, the Flight to Varennes, in June 1791, sent out the message that the King and Queen were unhappy and fearful for their future. On 19 July, Leopold II of Austria proposed an invasion of France via the Padua Circular, and on 27 August, Leopold and Frederick William II of Prussia published the Declaration of Pillnitz with the intention of restoring Louis and Marie-Antoinette to the French throne.

Throughout the early period of the revolution there were anti-Paris revolts in the provinces. These were generally small in scale and did not affect the progress of the revolution. But in 1793, with the outpouring of grievances in the West – in the Vendée – the Counter Revolution seemed to reinvent itself as a popular and threatening movement. Peasant bands, led by nobles, caused huge disruption. They were motivated by loyalty to Catholicism and the King and also powerful regional pride. It took the revolution the best part of two years to pacify the West, and even then this was not a permanent victory.

It is questionable how important ideas were in all of this. Of course, in the very early days of the revolution, Edmund Burke and Germaine de Staël had argued that it had broken with tradition and veered off dangerously into war and terror. And in 1796, Joseph de Maistre would publish his *Considerations on France*, a critique of the revolutionaries and their ideas, and also, at the same time, an affirmation of monarchy, religion and the role of providence in French history.

In this section we will evaluate the nature and significance of the Counter Revolution. What shape did it take? Was it about action or ideas? What did it believe in and was it an effective fighting force? We will first assess the role of the King and Queen in Paris; then we will consider the significance of the *émigrés* and the Vendée revolt; and finally we will examine the writings of Joseph de Maistre, probably the most famous spokesperson of the Counter Revolution.

King, Queen and Court

The nexus of the Counter Revolution was the Court. King and Queen, princes, courtiers – they all contributed to the atmosphere of plotting which held sway in Paris. For their part, Louis and Marie-Antoinette put up a façade. They went along with many aspects and facets of the revolution in public, but in private they were scheming. A contemporary onlooker surmised that the Court had a constitutional exterior and an anti-constitutional interior.

The King, obviously, was at the centre of things. For the best part of four years he maintained his position on the throne. He was not an unpopular monarch in some respects and always retained a belief in himself as the 'father figure' or 'figurehead' of the nation – whatever troubles and travails it was having to endure.

For this reason, Louis assumed full responsibility for some

key decisions. In 1791, he accepted the revolutionaries' first constitution and in 1792, he signed the decree which took France into war against Austria. In both contexts, the King was acting in a duplicitous manner. His acceptance of the constitution was bogus for at the royal session of 23 June 1789 he had made it be known – much to the delight of royalists such as Breteuil – that his ideal regime consisted of enlightened despotism moderated by only occasional constitutional concessions. (We should note that at this point in the revolution there was much discussion about the alternatives to absolute government; the partisans of absolute and constitutional monarchy were at loggerheads and the work of Edmund Burke was being used as a reference point by those interested in some kind of constitutional settlement.) The King's motives for declaring war were, also, anything but noble. He hoped that if the war went well he, as the man who officially instigated it, might take the accolades; and if it went badly, the expectation was that the edifice of the revolution would start to crumble – which could only be good for him.

At the same time, and very much in secret, the King was planning his own rescue. But he was playing a curious game. On 23 April 1791 he sent a circular to foreign courts via Montmorin, Minister of Foreign Affairs, implying that he had recognised the revolution:

> The ambassadors and ministers of France at all the courts of Europe are receiving the same orders, lest any doubt remain with regard to His Majesty's intentions, his free acceptance of the new form of government, or his irrevocable oath to maintain it. His Majesty convoked the Estates General of the kingdom and determined in his council that the commons should have therein a number of deputies equal to that of the other two orders then existing ... The Estates General assembled and took the title of National Assembly; soon a constitu-

tion, conducive to the happiness of France and of the monarch, supplanted the old regime in which the apparent force of royalty only concealed the real force of the abuses of some aristocratic bodies … What has the King not done to show that he counted the French Revolution and the Constitution also among his titles to glory?

However, by June 1791, having realised that his authority was much diminished, the King was ready to leave Paris.

The Flight to Varennes was the outcome. It was a failed effort to escape, and followed on from a number of other attempts to exit the capital with honour intact. The consequences of the Varennes episode were wholly negative for Louis. He 'died' in the eyes of his subjects – who were disappointed by his actions – and in time his prerogatives as king were withdrawn.

Ominously, too, the country was now divided, and it looked as if the monarchy had lost too much support. But still, Louis kept fighting: in November 1791 he vetoed a law which prescribed death for all *émigrés*. In short bursts and in irregular fashion he was determined to stand up to the revolution. This is why Cobban describes him as 'King at the same time of the Revolution and the Counter Revolution'. He was so obviously walking a tightrope – and in a sense it is more remarkable that he stayed on it for so long than that he actually lost his balance in the end.

Marie-Antoinette's position was similar but also slightly different. She not only shared Louis' concerns about the revolution, but displayed an intransigence that the King could not match. The key to understanding the Queen's position was her nationality. As an Austrian she had never been loved. Ordinary people felt they had little in common with her – and this feeling was exacerbated every time Marie-Antoinette uttered an insensitive word.

The perception was that an 'Austrian Committee' existed at the heart of the royal court, headed by Marie-Antoinette and involving a variety of French ambassadors and Old Regime loyalists. Whatever the reality, this perception took hold. There was talk of constant communication between the Court and foreign capitals, with the *émigrés* acting as intermediaries. This is where the Queen's Austrian heritage was so much of an issue. She had easy access to Vienna and was happy to exploit this.

The Padua Circular of 5 July 1791 is probably the best example of the Austrian royal family speaking on Marie-Antoinette's behalf. It was written by the Queen's brother, Emperor Leopold von Habsburg of Austria, in the aftermath of Varennes. As such, it makes reference to the 'unprecedented outrage of the arrest of the King of France, of my sister the Queen, and of the Royal Family'. The document is addressed to the monarchs of Europe:

> The most pressing [need] appears to be our immediate cooperation … having our ministers in France deliver a common declaration, or numerous similar and simultaneous declarations, which may curb the leaders of the violent party and forestall desperate decisions. This will still leave them an opportunity for honest repentance and for the peaceful establishment of a regime in France that will preserve at least the dignity of the crown and the essential requirements for general tranquillity.

The *émigrés*

It is a short step from talk of the Court to the *émigrés*, those who left France during the revolutionary period. Most, according to Bosher, were humble commoners – individuals who were simply trying to make new lives for themselves away from the political turbulence in France. But the most famous came from

the First and Second estates – those who were much more politically motivated. Anyone who left France during the revolutionary period was, technically, an *émigré*.

Greer and Vidalenc estimate that in total there were between
130,000 and 150,000 *émigrés*, which equated to 0.5 per cent of
the French population. The de facto leader of the *émigrés* was the
Comte d'Artois, the King's younger brother, but he had plenty
of support (if that is not flattering their role) in the shape of the
Comte de Provence (his older sibling), Calonne, the Duc de
Condé and the Comte d'Antraigues. Coblenz, in Prussia, was
their 'capital', but they also frequented the royal courts of
Venice, Vienna and London, as well as other major European
cities.

Roberts differentiates between '*émigrés* of disdain' and
'*émigrés* of fear'. The former were driven by ideology – whether
old-style absolutism or middle-of-the-road constitutionalism.
The latter were motivated by events – in particular, landmark
moments that seemed to spell the end for the monarchy (for
instance, the Civil Constitution of the Clergy, the Flight to
Varennes, the Constitution of 1791 and the execution of the
King).

What was the relationship between the King and the *émigrés*?
On one level they were close: the monarch's two brothers were
leading figures in the emigration and were bound by a common
outlook and value system. But on another level, relations were
poor. The King didn't trust the *émigrés* and communication was
imperfect. As if to demonstrate this, in December 1790 he was
forced to halt *émigré* plans to invade France from the south-east.

Nevertheless, the revolution was keen to drive a wedge
between the monarch and his followers at large. This was illustrated on 29 November 1791 when the revolutionaries
addressed the King: 'Sire, The National Assembly had no sooner
turned its gaze toward the state of the kingdom, than it noticed
that the continuing troubles have their source in the criminal

preparations of French *émigrés*. Their audacity is supported by the German princes who flout the treaties signed between themselves and France.' The address continued:

These preparations for hostilities and these threats of invasion require weapons that absorb immense sums that the nation would have gladly used to pay back its creditors. Sire, it is your role to make them stop. It is your role to address these foreign powers with a language worthy of the King of the French People. Tell them that wherever people allow preparations to be made against France, France shall view them as nothing less than enemies … Such as they are, let the hordes of *émigrés* be dissipated this instant ... Let your declaration be underscored by the movement of the forces that have been entrusted to you, so that the nation is aware of who are enemies and who are friends. With these bold steps, we shall recognise the defender of the Constitution. Thus you shall assure the serenity of the Empire, inseparable from your own. You shall also hasten the return of national prosperity, where peace shall bring back the order and reign of law, and where your happiness shall be mixed with that of all Frenchmen.

The tone of the revolutionaries is fascinating. Only sixteen months on from the Fall of the Bastille, they are now treating the King as an inferior: 'Tell them that …', 'Thus you shall assure …' The balance of power had certainly shifted.

In general terms, we could say that the *émigrés* personified the counter revolution at the 'top' of society. They saw themselves as a court-in-exile or court-in-waiting. This was not as fanciful as it sounds because they included in their ranks the future Louis XVIII and Charles X and a host of well-connected aristocrats. But they did not help themselves with their attitude. On his departure from France, the Comte d'Artois declared, 'We'll be back in three months.' It would, in fact, be twenty-five years before most of them returned. This sums up the *émigrés*: they were out of touch with reality.

Nevertheless, and highlighting perhaps the paranoia that was affecting Paris, the revolutionaries took the *émigrés* extremely seriously. They were not to know that as a body of men they were unusually lacking in strategy and political know-how. So they tried to legislate the *émigrés* out of existence, almost literally. Legislation was passed in 1791 and 1792 and then consolidated in a 'catch-all' decree on 28 March 1793. *Emigrés* were comprehensively defined as:

> 1st, Every French citizen, of either sex, who, having left the territory of the Republic since 1 July, 1789, has not given proof of his (or her) return to France within the time limits established by the decree of 30 March–8 April, 1792 ...
>
> 2nd, Every French citizen, of either sex, absent from the place of his (or her) domicile, who cannot give proof, in the form which is about to be prescribed, of continuous residence in France since 9 May, 1792;
>
> 3rd, Every French citizen of either sex, who, although now present, has absented himself (or herself) from the place of his (or her) domicile, and cannot give proof of continuous residence in France since 9 May, 1792 ...

Moreover, it was stipulated that *émigrés* were banished in perpetuity from France, they were to be regarded as dead and their property was to pass to the Republic. Those who attempted to re-enter French territory could be punished with death.

Clearly, nothing was being left to chance.

The Vendée rebellion

Most of the leading *émigrés* came from the Second Estate but, as we have seen, many of the non-political *émigrés* came from the

Third Estate and had little in common with the aristocrats and princes. Likewise with the Vendée. The vast majority of the rebels were peasants but, significantly, the leaders of the revolt came from the nobility. Historians have viewed the Vendée as the most important of the counter-revolutionary revolts. There were others – in the Midi, Brittany, Lyons, the south-west and the south-east – but the consensus is that the Vendée holds special significance for a number of reasons.

In March 1793 the Vendée reacted to the revolutionary government's attempt to impose conscription. Paris decreed that 300,000 men were required to fight for France and the revolution – and this proved unpopular. By July the Vendée had declared almost total independence from Paris. The rebels' fighting force – the Roman Catholic Army or Catholic and Royal Army – had besieged Nantes and was in control of most of the West.

Gradually, between late 1793 and 1795, Paris reasserted itself. The rebel army was destroyed in December 1793 and by the spring of 1795 treaties had been signed and the West pacified. But this was not the end. The Vendée was a running sore and erupted again in 1796, 1799, 1815 and 1832. But, to all intents and purposes, by 1795 Paris had dealt with the problem.

Why is the Vendée so significant as a revolt? This question can be answered in a number of ways. First, we have to return to the question of personnel. The anti-Paris coalition that emerged in the Vendée was an intriguing one. All three estates were represented: priests fearful of the revolution's policy on religion; nobles worried that their provincial powerbase was under threat; and peasants who disliked the idea of conscription. The common denominator was an attachment to the traditional way of life.

Second, the Vendée rebels came to be associated with a very distinctive type of warfare. Peasant brigands and terrorists – known as *Chouans* and made famous by Balzac's novel of the same name – started to roam the countryside. They engaged in a primitive form of warfare that took the revolutionaries by surprise. Paris was certainly kept informed of developments. On 25 August 1793 Choudieu, a local government official, sent this message to the National Convention:

> The departmental adviser reported to you, in the last mail, the troubling events which occurred in the district of Châtillon. New information shows us that the crowd is continuing to gather, that the leaders of bandits, far from scattering them, every day battle with them anew and retreat anew ... It is with the greatest of sorrow that we inform you that six patriots have already fallen victim to this rabble, but at least forty of their number were killed ... Having already dispatched all of the armed force that was at our disposal, the departments of the Vendée, Loire-Inférieure, and Maine-en-Loire showed us unequivocal proof of their fraternity and neighbourliness by coming to our aid during these circumstances. Without these departments, this unfortunate region would today have fallen to the rebels. We cannot hide from you sirs that a severe and swift example needs to be set. Already several of these bandits have been arrested, and the departmental adviser requests that you issue a decree whereby the criminal court of Niort judges this case as the last resort. It is the only way to bring peace back to this unfortunate region.

Here, the phrase 'unfortunate region' is used twice, as if emphasising the point that the Vendée was unique and also, perhaps, unlucky in the sense that 'misguided' individuals were besmirching its reputation and causing problems for the authorities in Paris.

Third, revolutionary propaganda portrayed the war in the Vendée as a battle between good and evil, 'virtue' and 'crime'. Fourth, the legacy of the rebellion has been immense. For more than two centuries, the Vendée has thrived on its reputation as a bastion of conservatism and Catholicism and an arch-opponent of radicalism and centralisation. As if to emphasise this, in 1989 the Vendée was the only French region to protest at Bicentennial celebrations.

Finally, the Vendée has fascinated historians because there is no consensus about origins and causation. The traditional view is that in its powerful attachment to religion and monarchism, the Vendée was unique among French regions. The fact that its main fighting force was christened the Catholic and Royal Army was indicative. It is argued that the region was passionately attached to its own identity and that the peasantry were happy to be led by their noble superiors.

But in recent times historians have taken a different perspective. Charles Tilly, in particular, has argued that the rebellion can best be explained in sociological terms. His thesis is that geography and topography hold the key to understanding the revolt. He concludes that the supporters of the uprising were from the parts of the region that were less fully integrated into regional markets than those parts in which support for the republic remained intact.

The ideas of Paul Bois, Tim Le Goff and Donald Sutherland should also be noted. They have shown that there were significant variations in the local settings in which support for, or opposition to, royalism occurred, and that these were linked to systems of land tenure, aspirations towards land ownership and the failure of successive legislatures to deal with these issues. Bois, for example, argues that it was the social surroundings of a person rather than his or her trade which determined his or her political attitudes.

Joseph de Maistre and the Theocrats

Joseph de Maistre existed on a different level to the King and Queen, the *émigrés* and the Vendée rebels. He was an aristocrat from Savoy (then part of Italy). He was a supporter of the revolution in its early years (1789–91), a lawyer by profession, and he understood the need for reform. But, when the revolution deteriorated into war and terror – from early 1792 onwards – he turned against it. He left Savoy for Russia and in 1796 published what has come to be viewed as the most famous counter-revolutionary treatise of all: *Considerations on France*.

In the book, de Maistre outlined his philosophy from first principles. Chapter 1 begins:

> We are all bound to the throne of the Supreme Being by a flexible chain which restrains without enslaving us. The most wonderful aspect of the universal scheme of things is the action of free beings under divine guidance. Freely slaves, they act at once of their own will and under necessity: they actually do what they wish without being able to disrupt general plans. Each of them stands at the centre of a sphere of activity whose diameter varies according to the decision of the eternal geometry, which can extend, restrict, check, or direct the will without altering its nature.

This passage sets the scene. Key ideas such as providence and divinity are introduced. He then goes on to contrast the works of man with the works of God. This is another significant idea in his political philosophy:

> In the works of man, everything is as poor as its author; vision is confined, means are limited, scope is restricted, movements are laboured, and results are humdrum. In divine works, boundless riches reveal themselves even in the smallest component; its power operates effortlessly: in its hands everything is pliant, nothing can resist it; everything is a means, nothing an obstacle: and the irregularities produced by the work of free agents come to fall into place in the general order. If one

imagines a watch all of whose springs continually vary in power, weight, dimension, form, and position, and which nevertheless invariably shows the right time, one can get some idea of the action of free beings in relation to the plans of the Creator. In the political and moral world, as in the physical, there is a usual order and there are exceptions to this order. Normally, we see a series of effects following the same causes; but in certain ages we see usual effects suspended, causes paralysed and new consequences emerging. A miracle is an effect produced by a divine or superhuman cause which suspends or is inconsistent with an ordinary cause. If in the middle of winter a man, before a thousand witnesses, orders a tree to cover itself suddenly with leaves and fruit, and if the tree obeys, everyone will proclaim a miracle.

As can be seen, de Maistre's writings are heavily laden with religious language and imagery. It was his way of countering the 'upstart' ideas of the revolution. As such, he is often labelled a 'theocrat', a thinker who like Bonald and Chateaubriand conceived of the fight against the revolution in primarily religious terms.

So the question has to be asked. What was counter-revolutionary about de Maistre? Clearly, he had deep reservations about the course of the revolution. He had been affected personally by the war – the revolutionary armies had entered Savoy and he had been forced to flee. He also looked on at the Terror with disdain. He was offended by the anarchy that it brought and equated those in charge to 'barbarians'. De Maistre took a particular dislike to the religious terror. He condemned the revolutionaries' attempts to create a new religion and saw in the destruction of church buildings an evil agenda at work.

Likewise, *Considerations on France* opposes the ideas of the Enlightenment. It portrays the *philosophes* as dangerous individuals, determined to spread their decadent and destabilising ideas with the ultimate goal of undermining the French body politic. What is more, de Maistre ridiculed the notion that political constitutions could be manufactured by men rather than God. This, to him, was preposterous. He also poked fun at the efforts of revolutionary leaders to make legislation. The irony of course was that he himself was an intellectual, a man of ideas, although he would not have wanted to admit this fact.

Religion was central to de Maistre's political views. Although he was not a devout believer himself, his mother had grown up in the Church and he had been imbued with a respect and reverence for the Christian religion. So, his political doctrine rested on two main pillars. First, providence: this could be defined as a kind of 'religious fate'. According to de Maistre, God had willed the revolution to 'punish' France for her crimes – for example, the lack of meaningful political reform and the extravagance of the Court. Here we should note that, unlike others on the right, de Maistre was a realist: he knew that reform was needed and also that the country could never go back to untrammelled absolutism. But, at the same time, he passionately believed that, some time in the future, providence would restore the French kings via a counter revolution. Second, theocracy: a new but old system of government. De Maistre's ideal regime was a fatherly Christian monarchy. One of his works was entitled *Pope and Executioner* – and he assigned great importance to these two jobs. The Pope, obviously, would stand at the apex of the political/religious system. Meanwhile, 'Executioner' was a euphemism and hinted at stronger law and order.

Overall, de Maistre exhibited a belief in the natural order and traditionalism. In his view, hierarchy, inequality and monarchy were sanctioned by God. Of course, this theocratic vision of society is open to attack. It is difficult to entertain a set of political ideas that rest so intrinsically on religious faith. The belief in providence, for example, is almost impossible to argue with: you either believe in it or not. How can de Maistre prove that the revolution and counter revolution (if it ever actually occurred) were the work of God rather than man? Should he not give more weight to factors such as class, social change and economics?

In a sense, de Maistre personified the Counter Revolution. There was a will and a determination, but in the end little to show for it. Naturally, the King and Queen were the focal-point but they were hamstrung by their own problems and their lack of room for manoeuvre. The *émigrés* and the Vendée rebels had the potential to cause problems for the revolution, but they never achieved enough on their own or in tandem. Now the question was: how would the revolution proceed in the aftermath of the Terror?

7

The Thermidorian Reaction: 1794–95

Welcome, Nine Thermidor, day of delivery
You have come to purify a bloody land
For the second time
You make France glisten
The rays of Liberty
In two days you have avenged
The disgrace of our fathers
But the scepter fallen
From the hands of the final king
Rearmed the people's tyrants
Only you could destroy him
Only you could destroy him.

> Hymn commemorating the overthrow of Robespierre
> and the Committee of Public Safety, 27 July 1794

Narrative overview: deportations and insurrections

The phase of the revolution known as the Thermidorian Reaction spanned fifteen months between July 1794 and November 1795. The 'men of Thermidor' emerged in the aftermath of the fall of Robespierre on 27–28 July (9–10 Thermidor) 1794.

The first objective was to reorganise the government. With this in mind, the Law of 22 Prairial (10 June 1794) – establishing the Reign of Terror – was reversed and the Revolutionary Tribunal reorganised. The early months of Thermidor also witnessed an outpouring of vigilante justice known as the 'White Terror'. In Paris, the reactionary *jeunesse dorée* (or guilded youth) was renowned for its thuggish behaviour; its well-to-do members engaged in random acts of violence against left-wing militants. At the same time, in Lyon and the South, pro-Thermidor forces followed a strategy of purges and massacres.

The new regime had to contend with a bout of huge price inflation and a series of risings in Paris in the early spring of 1795. On 1 September 1794, Billaud, Barère and Collot left the Committee of Public Safety, and on the 18 September, the regime ended all subsidies to religion – a statement of intent regarding the religious terror. Five months later, on 21 February 1795, freedom of worship was restored.

In November, the Thermidorians had the Jacobin Club closed, and in December they abolished the Maximum – the centrepiece of the economic terror of 1793–94. In the same month, they reinstated those Girondins who had survived the Terror and put the radical Jacobin, Jean-Baptiste Carrier, on trial and executed him. There was little love lost between the left and the new regime. On 12 Germinal (1 April 1795), Thermidor had to fend off a Jacobin insurrection; and on 1 Prairial (20 May 1795), it had to deal with a rising of ordinary men and women demanding 'Bread and the Constitution of 1793'.

The leaders of the regime were able to pacify La Jaunaye in February 1795 – a key achievement given the troubles previous revolutionary regimes had encountered in the West. In April, the Thermidorians concluded a peace with the Chouans at La Prévalaye, and in July, Paris defeated the *émigrés* at Quiberon – another landmark event in the history of relations with the Counter Revolution.

In foreign policy, Thermidor was committed to peace. In April 1795 France signed the Peace of Basle with Prussia, in May the Treaty of The Hague with Holland, and in July the Treaty of Basle with Spain.

An anti-Jacobin coalition

Thermidor (or Fervidor) was the second month of summer in the new revolutionary calendar. The word came from the Greek *thermos* meaning 'heat'. Over the course of the revolution, many individual months came to be associated with significant revolutionary events, but only one became synonymous with a regime: Thermidor. Essentially, this was the end of the 'radical' revolution of 1793–94. Thermidor lasted fifteen months, from July 1794 to November 1795, and can be seen as the harbinger of the Directory.

Who were the men of Thermidor, those who came to be known as the Thermidorians? In the main they were individuals who had previous, passionate loyalties: ex-Dantonists, ex-*enragés* and even a scattering of ex-Jacobins. But there were also a number of people who defined themselves by their opposition to the Jacobins, and this became a recurring theme. Important Thermidorians included Louis-Marie Stanislas Fréron, Paul François Jean Nicolas Barras, Jean-Lambert Tallien and Joseph Fouché. Another key figure was René Levasseur. In his memoirs he portrays a regime that was in tune with the early revolution but was also slightly unpredictable:

> We have arrived at the moment when the revolution, having reached its apogee, is going to turn back. It was time no doubt for the revolutionary regime to cease, but for the principles of the revolution to lose nothing thereby, it had to be stopped by its own children ... a Danton or a Robespierre ... It

was not so. To consummate the resolution of 9 thermidor, its authors addressed themselves to all the parties even to the men who, after 31 May [1793], had become the enemies of the Republic: their fatal support made of 9 thermidor a veritable reaction ... We saw a coalition, composed of the most disparate elements, overturn Robespierre's party. It was impossible to foresee what would be the result of a victory won by such a coalition.

What is significant here is the depiction of the men of Thermidor as 'a coalition, composed of the most disparate elements'. This substantiates the point made earlier. Essentially, the Thermidorians were a broad coalition, with little in common except an instinct that was passionately anti-Jacobin.

Levasseur's accusation notwithstanding, the Thermidorians' approach was consistent at home and abroad. They wanted peace in Paris, where the revolution had spiralled out of control during the Terror; they wished to pacify the West, where opposition to the revolution was widespread; and they were serious about pursuing peace initiatives across Europe. But, at home and abroad, they were pragmatic enough to bend their own rules occasionally.

At home it would not be exaggerating the situation to say that the men of Thermidor were paranoid about any sign of the Terror being rekindled. This point is made very strongly by Doyle. He says that, more than anything else, Thermidor marked a rejection of the form of rule associated with Robespierre: Revolutionary Government, the Maximum and the guillotine. The guillotine had emerged as the symbol *par excellence* of the Terror and the instinct of the Thermidorians was to ban its use forthwith. This they did, releasing suspects, returning sequestrated property to the individuals concerned, and also doing away with other apparatus of the Jacobin period.

The fall of Robespierre: a personal vendetta

On 10 June 1794, a new piece of legislation was passed: the Law of 22 Prairial (also known as the *loi de la Grande Terreur*). This led to an extensive categorisation of suspects and an increase in the number of public executions. Within two months, Robespierre and his associates were murdered in what Cobban has labelled the 'biggest single Holocaust of the revolution'. Between twenty and seventy radical revolutionaries met their death in this impromptu purge, and the policy of murder continued into August and the last months of the year, with fifty or more political executions taking place on the orders of the new administration. This period of killing came to be known as the White Terror: the men of Thermidor taking their revenge on the Robespierreists by using the system of terror instituted by the latter.

On 8 Thermidor – the day before Robespierre was guillotined – Jean-Marie Collot d'Herbois, a member of the Committee of Public Safety, spoke at the Jacobin Club: '[He] began to speak with great energy; he needed the full force of his lungs to make heard his suspicions about Robespierre's intentions.' What comes through from contemporary sources is the level of hostility that Robespierre engendered as an individual. Of course, there was a political battle going on, as there had been since the early period of the revolution, between the ideas of the Girondins and Jacobins. But for many it was also, unquestionably, a personal vendetta. For one observer:

Robespierre had become unbearable, even to his own accomplices. The members of the committees were in a power struggle with him, and were afraid that sooner or later, they would become his victims. When faced with his tyranny in the Convention, everyone whimpered, not daring to attack him ...

> Every tyrant who threatens but does not strike is himself struck. Tallien, Bourdon and two or three other Montagnards who had been threatened could no longer sleep, so, to defend themselves, they formed a conspiracy against Robespierre.

Here, the implication is that the anti-Robespierre coup that eventually took place – Thermidor – was a pre-emptive strike.

There was certainly drama in the convention hall on 27 July 1794. One account has it that:

> Robespierre went up to the rostrum to defend Saint-Just. The only words that could be heard were: 'Down with the tyrant! Arrest him!' Since the Mountain was still acting alone, Robespierre turned ... and said: 'Deputies of the Right, men of honour, men of virtue, give me the floor, since the assassins will not.' He hoped to receive this favour as a reward for the protection he had given us. But our party was decided. There was no answer, just dead silence until the debate over the decree to arrest Robespierre and his accomplices, for which we all voted in favour, which made the decision unanimous.

On reflection, it could be argued that Robespierre's downfall was inevitable. He had created a system – the Terror – that was now out of control.

Those who were eventually responsible for Robespierre's death came from within the revolutionary government. Some were motivated by the need for self-preservation; others by political motives. There was almost unanimous support for his arrest and the National Convention had no option but to order it. News of the dictator's demise was quick to spread. Two days on from the guillotining, a letter to Laffitte, executive officer of the district administration at Saint-Sever, stated:

> Robespierre has gone to join Camille Desmoulins. He was guillotined yesterday with Saint-Just, Le Bas, and Couthon ... For a month Robespierre had not attended the meetings of the

Committee of Public Safety and this antagonised people more
... The assembly, already very irritated, enacted the decree for
his arrest ... We finally had the sense to take some measures
instead of declaiming to one another that we had to die at our
post ... Robespierre was abandoned, and he is no more! It is
too bad, for the Republic, that this event can be counted
among the great events. The death of one man in a free state
ought to make no commotion. We shall now have to wait
several days to know what course events will take. I very much
wish it were clear that we knew how to take advantage of
liberty and that passions would cool.

The tone of this letter (from an unknown source) was indicative
of Thermidorian thinking on a general plane: minimising the
significance of the death of one man and hoping that 'passions
would cool'. In objective terms, this is also what France
required. The mood was certainly changing. Thermidor had
ushered in a new set of policies and political climate. Doyle talks
about a drop in executions, a release of suspects and, in general
terms, an 'outburst of relief'.

At home and abroad

Robespierre might have been dispensed with but key institutions – the Convention and the Committee of Public Safety –
remained. They were a shadow of their former selves, though.
In the words of Louis-Marie de La Révellière-Lepaux, a
Thermidor-era politician, 'The Convention was no longer the
formidable assembly that it was ... it was nothing more than a
spineless mob, a mass without cohesion, formed from the
incoherent remnants of all the parties that had been successively
removed and destroyed.' Meanwhile:

The Committee of Public Safety, the true heart of the State and
the only pillar onto which to hold, which alone could rally

everyone and move them to action, had itself fallen into complete dissolution. Although I had been warned about this deplorable state, as soon as I saw the committee first-hand I thought I was entering the grave, buried under the rubble of France. I felt the most acute anguish that only a true friend of the homeland could feel when he sees it swallowed by the abyss. The committee members only concerned themselves with their own business, or with the business of their friends or supporters.

The implication here was that corruption had taken hold, and the post-Thermidor regime, the Directory, would have to face up to the same charge.

The men of Thermidor were soon busy. On 24 August, sixteen new committees were set up to fill the void left by the Committee of Public Safety and Committee of General Security. On 7 September, the Maximum was extended, but only temporarily. On the eighteenth the new administration ended all subsidies to religion – a key break with the Robespierre regime, which had committed itself to a new state-sponsored deity. And on 24 September the rebels of Ile-et-Vilaine were offered an amnesty – exemplifying the Thermidorians' desire for domestic peace.

Towards the end of the year there were landmarks in the war on radicalism. On 12 November the Jacobin Club was closed and on 24 December the Maximum was abolished. This was the period of the White Terror, with the regime determined to expunge all traces of Jacobinism from the French body politic. At the same time, it was encouraging a new brand of moderate politics; and this was illustrated on 8 December when the Girondin politicians ousted on 2 June 1793 were allowed back into the Convention.

The attack on extremism, of all forms, continued into 1795. On 8 February, the remains of Marat – one of the heroes of the radical revolution – were burned and then thrown away, indicating that his memory was no longer held in esteem; on 2 April a popular uprising in Paris, caused by the removal of price ceilings, was crushed; and on 10 April a law was passed disarming Jacobin terrorists and forbidding them to organise. But it was impossible to prohibit all radical activity. The Jacobins continued to organise and cause problems for the regime. In the end the Thermidorians resorted to force: in May they massacred a group of them imprisoned in Lyon and in June they used the same tactics against diehard Robespierre supporters in Marseille.

The hatred of Jacobinism was real but the Thermidorians were aware of the achievements of the Robespierre era. This was particularly the case in education. The Jacobins had put forward the idea of universal education and the Thermidorians built on this. On 17 November 1794 they introduced a system of public primary education that impressed many people. The decree introduced primary education for both girls and boys, providing 'the instruction necessary for free peoples', in schools throughout the Republic at the rate of one school for every 1,000 inhabitants.

The decree went on to stipulate that the teachers 'shall be chosen by the people; nevertheless, throughout the duration of the Revolutionary Government, they shall be examined, selected, and supervised by a jury of instruction, composed of three members designated by the district administration, and chosen from among the fathers of families of the district.'

Clearly, in itself, this piece of legislation was significant. It also reveals much about the mentality of Thermidor as a regime. The rationality and logic present in the plans for the schools appears to echo early revolutionary decrees on administration and other matters, while the idea of 'instruction' and 'teachers ... chosen by the people' has echoes of the radical period. The fact that Thermidor is still using the phrase 'Revolutionary Government' is also interesting; although its central objective is moderation and stability, it is obviously happy to align itself with other post-1789 regimes.

On foreign policy, the Thermidorians' common-sense outlook told them that it was time to call a halt to the various conflicts and regroup. So, in April 1795, France and Prussia signed the Peace of Basle; in May a ceasefire was agreed with the Netherlands; and in July France and Spain signed a peace. By necessity, the Thermidorians were also interested in securing peace at home. In July 1795 a major step was taken in this direction when the *émigrés*, who had invaded France in support of the Vendée rebels, were defeated at the Battle of Quiberon. Thereafter, Thermidor was focused on constitutional matters. In August 1795 what became known as the Constitution of the Year III was voted. This legal arrangement heralded the birth of the Directory, whose rule officially began in November.

'Drab' and 'unpopular'?

How has Thermidor been interpreted? Cobban argues that the Thermidorians had little in common. They 'were united only in their fear of Robespierre,' he says. For Rudé, taking a longer-term perspective, the prognosis was not good: 'The fall of Robespierre led to something of an anti-climax. The Revolution continued, though at a slackened pace; and the Republic – a new "republic of proprietors" – lingered on through a series of crises.' Sutherland, meanwhile, articulates another view: 'If the Revolution was a genuinely popular revolution, the argument goes, then the destruction of a popular government on 9–10 thermidor or, alternatively, the defeat of the *sans-culottes* in germinal-prairial AN III, marked the end of the Revolution.'

As we have already stated, Thermidor is a fifteen-month phase of the revolution that is easily – indeed often – overlooked.

Furthermore, those historians who do take it seriously are not overflowing in their praise. Woronoff, for example, calls it a 'drab interlude', 'history in a minor key' and an administration whose only achievement was 'a new equilibrium' between rival forces. In fact, a common view is that the Thermidor regime was so lacking in everything that it is fitting that it was named after nothing more exciting than the month in which it emerged.

Neither did it have the common touch. The widespread perception was that the middle classes, who had steered the revolution through the period 1789–92 and lost influence when the revolution veered off into popular politics and the Terror, came again in the post-Robespierre period. Rudé is actually quite cynical, arguing that the Thermidorians were 'hard-headed men, to whom the Revolution had been a profitable business; it had given them authority and status; many had been enriched by the purchase of "national properties", others by lucrative government contracts.' Thus, it would be a mistake to think that Thermidor – however anonymous its leaders and mundane its objectives – appealed to ordinary people in any meaningful way. It existed and survived for fifteen months but, as is obvious from the fact that a new constitution was unveiled in August 1795, it saw itself as nothing more than a prelude to the Directory.

In fact, one could argue that as a regime it was unpopular. Both the left and the right took exception to it. The Parisian *sans-culottes* particularly disliked it. After all, they stood for regulation and a command economy – the type that had ruled France during the terror years – whereas Thermidor, as part of its effort to steer the country back to the values of 1789, stood for liberal economics and free trade. Gendron considers this theme in his book, *Gilded Youth of Thermidor*. His argument is that under Thermidor the *sans-culottes* lost out to a rival faction, the *jeunesse dorée* or 'gilded youth', who patrolled the streets in the post-Robespierre period looking to 'out' unreformed Jacobins. As Gilroy has written, 'These sons of the bourgeoisie were violently anti-Jacobin in their political philosophy … In ideology and life-style they were the very antithesis of the *sans-culottes*, and the mutual antagonism between the two groups was as deep as their differences.'

So, Thermidor did not placate the left. Neither did it ingratiate itself to the right. On 13 Vendémiaire – 5 October 1795 – the royalists revolted over the so-called 'law of two-thirds'. This piece of legislation stated that two-thirds of the members of the new legislature would be taken from the membership of the Convention – a clear indication that the Thermidorians wished to stay in power and minimise the royalist threat. Consequently, the forces of the right felt betrayed. They saw no future in Thermidor and little prospect of a royalist restoration. A lone Thermidorian, Boissy d'Anglas, made it be known that he was cautiously in favour of a return to constitutional monarchy, but that was the sum total of pro-royalist feeling and it did little to assuage those on the right who speculated that the coming of Thermidor was good news for the monarchist cause. In the end, Vendémiaire was put down by a young general by the name of Napoleon Bonaparte.

There are other theories too. One says that Thermidor was a reaction; in effect, the end of the revolution. This makes some sense, but only up to a point. Various histories of the revolution only take the story up to 1794, as if Thermidor lacked a basic, prerequisite revolutionary ingredient. It is the case, certainly, that the Thermidorians were devoid of a vision, unlike the revolutionaries of 1789, the liberals of 1789–92 and the Jacobins of 1792–94, who all had (albeit very different) radical agendas.

Probably a more convincing view is that 1794 heralded a return to the values of 1789. Five years had passed, the revolution had radicalised after a liberal beginning, and the coming to power of the Thermidorians marked a U-turn that was both necessary and applauded by most political moderates. The language of the Thermidorians themselves lends credence to this view. For Pierre-Toussaint Durand-Maillane, a member of the Convention in 1794–95:

> Every honest man should want that the freedom of opinion never be jeopardised by unproven charges or invective. We should not swear at men whom we look upon as 'weak beings' in order to shackle the opinions that they only want to express for the good of the People. If someone here believes that they should make a serious reproach toward one of his colleagues, let him explain himself and stipulate the facts, not just offer insults. Let the accused be heard, and let us not seek to make people fear from threats. Only the conspirators should be afraid.

It was as if the revolution had turned full circle. In this respect it is perhaps also significant that the *Marseillaise* was unveiled as the French National Anthem on 14 July 1795.

Another interpretation stresses the human dimension to Thermidor. It was about paranoia, ending the horrors of the terror, and emphasising the value of moderation over extremism. In a word: survival. Levasseur admits as much: 'The Thermidorians had no fixed opinions, no settled doctrines. They studied public opinion in order to conform to it, and all their acts were the result of outside influence. Thus, when it was clear that moderation was the general desire, they paraded moderation.' In fact, some critics would argue that this was the only thing that unified the men of Thermidor.

Finally, the opposition to Thermidor. What does this say about the regime? With the Jacobin dictatorship fresh in the memory, it was never going to be easy for the Thermidorians. What is more, the Maximum was no longer in operation and ordinary folk were suffering as a result. Bread riots were commonplace and there was much disquiet and discontent at the bottom of society. On a political level, the threat from the left had not subsided. This forced the Thermidorians into violence – what came to be known as the 'White Terror'.

But protest and opposition continued. In May 1795 a group of radical women converged on the Convention Hall. They saw Thermidor as a middle-class, propertied regime and demanded that the (stillborn) Jacobin constitution of 1793 be implemented. They caused such an outcry that other, more moderate-minded, women felt a duty to denounce them to the authorities. This is the testimony of one such woman, Anne Marguerite Andelle of rue des Fosses:

> The voice of duty imperiously orders all ordinary individuals, above all in the crises we are in, to denounce enemies of the public interest, to make them known, and to establish a line of demarcation between them and respectable people. Consequently, I declare that I saw the above-named Femme Periot, a merchant at one of the gates of the Louvre, residing on rue des Lavandières, at the hatter's house next to the baker's – I declare, I say, that I saw the above-named, long before the Prairial Days, constantly showing loyalty to the Jacobin system, preaching Marat's maxims to various groups, and repeatedly demanding that heads roll. I saw her at the trial of Carrier conspiring on behalf of the Jacobins at the Revolutionary Tribunal. She was always threatening the Convention with an imminent dissolution and merchants with certain pillage. Revolted by the conduct of this shrew, I have denounced her to the Committee of Police of the Convention.

Of course, the Thermidorians wanted to establish a new kind of politics, and take apart the infrastructure of the Terror, but it is interesting that as late as May 1795 'denunciations' were still being received by the Committee of Police of the Convention.

It is natural for historians to describe Thermidor as an 'interlude', 'stepping stone' or 'transitionary regime'. It came after the Terror and before the Directory – in fact it could be argued that its *raison d'être* was to prepare the way, politically and constitutionally, for a Directory-esque regime to emerge. A balanced conclusion would say that the Thermidorian Reaction was shortlived and lacking in drama, but also significant in the longer term.

8

The Directory: 1795–99

The house of every citizen is an inviolable asylum; during the night no-one shall have the right to enter except in case of fire, flood, or a call proceeding from inside the house ... Corporations and associations which are contrary to public order may not be formed ... No assembly of citizens may call itself a popular society. No private society which concerns itself with political questions may correspond with another, or affiliate therewith, or hold public sessions ... or cause its members to wear any external insignia of their association.

Constitution of 1795

Narrative overview: from Babeuf to the Consulate

The rule of the Directory began in November 1795. In February 1796, the *assignat* was abolished, and in March, Napoleon Bonaparte was appointed military commander in Italy. In May, the Directors had to contend with the Babeuf Conspiracy – a threat from the left instigated by Gracchus Babeuf, a Rousseau-inspired radical. He was arrested, put on trial and eventually executed. Abroad there were victories at Lodi, Arcola, and (in January 1797) Rivoli.

For much of 1797, the Directory had to concern itself with the royalist threat. In April, constitutional monarchists made gains in partial elections. Then, on 4 September (18 Fructidor), a pre-emptive coup was launched against the royalist right. As part of their efforts to stabilise the French economy, the Directory also returned to a metallic currency. In July, they instituted a reorganisation of government and also shut down various political clubs. In August, they repealed the laws against the clergy.

In 1798, the Directory passed a new electoral law (January) and also staged new elections (March). In political terms, the regime was threatened by the left. This explains the passing of the Law of 22 Floréal (11 May), which annulled key elections and also deprived dozens of left-wing deputies of their seats in the Council of Five Hundred – the lower house of the French legislature.

Following a wave of military and diplomatic successes, France signed the Treaty of Campo Formio on 17 October 1797. This marked the failure of the First Coalition – the combined efforts of Austria, Prussia and Great Britain – to contain France. In 1798, the Egyptian expedition was approved. It commenced in May, with Napoleon Bonaparte landing in Egypt in July. France was involved in the Battle of the Pyramids (21 July) and the Battle of the Nile (1 August), with Nelson's victory at the latter resulting in thousands of French casualties and having negative implications for Napoleon in Egypt.

In June 1799, the French were defeated by the Austrians and Russians at the Battle of the Trebia in northern Italy. In the same month, the (bloodless) coup of 30 Prairial removed the Directors and left Abbé Sieyès as the major figure in government. Napoleon left Egypt on 24 August and returned to France on 9 October. Exactly a month later, on 9 November, the end of the Directory was officially proclaimed after the coup of 18 Brumaire. On 24 December, the Constitution of the Year VIII was published, heralding the Consulate of Napoleon I and it is at this juncture that most historians consider the French Revolution to have ended.

Moderation and stability

The Directory was an antidote to terror. This was its philosophy and *raison d'être*. After the radicalisation of the revolution in the period 1792–94, the men the Directory styled themselves as beacons of moderation and stability. They were scared of a return to extremism – of the left or right.

Traditionally, historians have been unkind to the Directory. Hobsbawm, for example, argues that the regime had no genuine political support; rather, it was tolerated. Others have claimed that it lacked vision, aimed merely at survival, pleased nobody and, what is more, was elitist and corrupt while in power.

But this section will try and balance the debate by examining the positive as well as the negative features of the administration. Should we not congratulate the Directory for surviving for four years – a significant achievement in the context of revolutionary politics? For returning the country to moderation and stability? For honouring the values of 1789 and the early revolution? In general terms, how should we interpret the Directory? Simply as a response to the Terror? Or a calculated exercise in reaction? Or, actually, as a regime that tried to consolidate key aspects of the revolution?

The relationship between Thermidor and the Directory is crucial. The men of Thermidor saw themselves as laying the foundations for another, more permanent, regime. The constitution of the Directory, published in August 1795, seemed to be the outcome of their work. Essentially, the Directors were aiming to restore the ethos of 1789, rather than 1793. As such, they wanted property – rather than equality – to be the centrepiece of their regime.

The two main features of the Directory were its five-man executive and its bicameral legislature. Neither bore much relation to the principles of 1789 but both fitted well-established models of ancient republican government (such as those, for example, in Rome and Sparta). Unlike in the United States, there was no president. In fact, those who established the Directory did everything possible to avoid a concentration of power in one person, fearful as they were of another Robespierre-type figure emerging. In a more general sense it should be pointed out that, in the late eighteenth century, there was little, if any, agreement on what a republican system of government should look like, mainly because there were so few republics actually in existence.

The Constitution of August 1795, also known as the Constitution of Year III, has fascinated historians. It began:

> The Executive Power shall be delegated to a Directory of five members appointed by the Legislative Body … The members of the Directory must be at least forty years of age. They may be chosen only from among citizens who have been ministers or members of the Legislative Body … The Directory shall be renewed in part by the election of one new member annually. During the first four years, the order of retirement of those first elected shall be determined by lot. None of the retiring members may be re-elected until after an interval of five years.

This careful approach – the caveats about age and re-election, for example – was symptomatic of the Directory. It was a 'safety first' document that returned political power to the middle classes after the horrors of the Terror. Again, as if returning to the ways of 1789, the law was pre-eminent:

> Laws and acts of the Legislative Body shall be addressed to the Directory in the person of its president … The Directory shall provide, according to law, for the external and internal security of the Republic. It may issue proclamations in conformity with the laws, and for the execution thereof … It shall supervise and ensure the execution of laws in the administrations and courts,

through commissioners of its own appointment … The law shall recognise neither religious vows nor any obligation contrary to the natural rights of man … No one may be held responsible for what he has written or published, except in cases provided for by law … The law shall watch particularly over the professions which affect public morals and the security and health of citizens … The law shall provide for the compensation of inventors, or for the maintenance of the exclusive ownership of their discoveries or productions.

Just as the early phase of the revolution had been dominated by lawyers with a belief in legality, so, after a period of anarchy and lawlessness, the Directory was trying to restore the rule of law.

Mindful of the excesses of the Robespierre era, the Directors did not wish for a high profile. Over the course of four years a number of men served in this role, including Étienne-François Le Tourneur, François Barthélemy, François de Neufchâteau, Jean-Baptiste Treilhard, Louis-Jérôme Gohier, Lazare Carnot, Philippe-Antoine Merlin, Jean-François-Auguste Moulin, Jean-François Rewbell, Pierre-Roger Ducos, Paul Barras and Louis-Marie de La Révellière. And it would be fair to say that only Emmanuel-Joseph Sieyès, on account of his pamphlet, *What is the Third Estate?*, had any kind of profile before serving on the Directory.

On 5 November 1795, the Directors spoke directly to the people: 'Frenchmen, the Executive Directory has just been installed. Resolved to maintain liberty or to perish, it is determined to consolidate the Republic and to give all dispatch and vigour to the Constitution.' This passage emphasises the republicanism of the regime, and its belief in order, but the first line was not promising. The Directory has been 'installed' – not 'elected' or 'welcomed in power by popular acclaim'. 'Installed' would seem to be a very functional word, as if the Directory, in a fairly matter-of-fact way, was 'filling a gap'. This reputation would stay with it for most of its time in power.

In talking about their aims, the Directors went on to emphasise their republican credentials:

> To wage an active war on royalism, to revive patriotism, to repress all factions vigorously, to destroy all party spirit, to annihilate every desire for vengeance, to establish concord, to restore peace, to regenerate morals, to reopen the sources of production, to revive commerce and industry, to stifle speculation, to revivify the arts and sciences, to re-establish plenty and the public credit, to reinstate social order in place of the chaos which is inseparable from revolutions, finally, to obtain for the French Republic the happiness and glory which awaits … Frenchmen … support with wisdom the ever active efforts and the imperturbable progress of the Executive Directory towards the prompt establishment of public happiness; and soon, with the glorious title of Republicans, you will irrevocably assure national peace and prosperity.

This is interesting because some observers – at the time and later – have questioned the political orientation of the regime. Surely, they suggest, the Directory was the end of the revolution? The point at which radicalism ended and reaction began? As such, could the Directory be equated to counter-revolution? Was the republic actually under threat? There are no straightforward answers to these questions. But it is clear that, on the whole, the Directory had little sympathy with monarchism or counter-revolution. Of course, the regime was counter-revolutionary in the sense that it wanted to deradicalise the revolution, but to say that it was counter-revolutionary in the sense that it wanted a return to monarchy would be completely misleading. Anyway, monarchism was going out of fashion. The *émigrés* were viewed as extreme and untrustworthy (for this reason it was announced, 'The property of *émigrés* is irrevocably acquired for the benefit of the Republic'), and the peasantry – the bastion of the Old

Regime – were adapting themselves to changed circumstances and did not want to go back to the inequities of feudalism.

It would also be fair to say that, as a period, the Directory is slightly under-researched and underplayed by historians. This links to a number of factors. In essence, the Directory was an extension of Thermidor and, as such, the two regimes are often bracketed together (with neither perhaps receiving the appropriate attention). Also, the period 1795–99 is sandwiched between two 'epic' eras: the Terror and Napoleon. This has meant that, in the rush to locate heroic personalities and drama, the Directory has often been neglected. Of course, it did not help itself in this respect. It came to power wishing to limit the power of individual politicians, and this it achieved spectacularly.

It should be noted that the Directory attracted a range of supporters and critics. Benjamin Constant and Germaine de Staël were friends. The former wrote in support of the regime and – by implication – in opposition to the Counter Revolution, while the latter, who was of the acquaintance of key figures in the regime, argued that, whatever its defects, the Directory had raised France from a 'deplorable situation', particularly in the sphere of economics. But Sieyès was an opponent. He disliked the Constitution of 1795 and initially refused to serve as a Director.

We should remind ourselves that the Directory came to power with a sensible and noble aim: to create order and stability and to sideline extremists on both left and right. And we should judge it on this.

Domestic policy: elections and economics

The Constitution of 1795 set the agenda for the Directory's domestic policy. If the aim was stability, moderation and a return to liberal, 1789-style politics, the means revolved around elections. The Directory was passionate about the need to be seen to be acting in as democratic a manner as possible. Given the horrors of the Terror this was understandable.

As late as 4 March 1799, Nicolas-Louis François de Neufchâteau, twice Minister of the Interior under the Directory, was exhorting local officials to take the democratic process seriously:

> Citizen commissioners, the approaching elections impose important tasks upon you, and I am going to speak to you about them ... It is up to you ... who are the guardians of the Government, to demonstrate the misfortunes to which they [citizens] are exposing themselves should they allow themselves to be influenced by factions. Never stop telling them of the sacred clause in our basic laws, the clause that reminds them that it is the soundness of choice in the primary and electoral assemblies upon which the duration, preservation, and prosperity of the Republic primarily depends.

Overall, historians are sceptical about the Directory's credentials in this area. There is no doubt that the regime wished to be perceived as being overtly democratic, but the reality was that it paid lip service to elections and engaged in a variety of crude and corrupt practices (including cancelling polls and using the army to clamp down on dissent).

On the economy, the Directory has had to face a range of criticisms. With the end of the Terror, the switch from control and regulation to a more relaxed economic environment was never going to be easy. The main problem was the currency, the *assignat*. In 1795, it was worth just one per cent of face value, and by 1796, it had totally collapsed. The stories told about France in this period resemble the famous ones about Weimar Germany: a printing-house floor collapsed because of the amount of *assignat*s that had been printed, and the worthlessness of the currency forced the authorities to pay the Directors their salaries in kind – in the form of grain.

There were other related problems: spiralling inflation and a political and economic system at the mercy of speculators; an unbalanced budget and problems relating to the collection of taxation; growing poverty and a famine induced by the disappointing harvest of 1795; and a general economic and trading situation which was hampered internally by political instability and externally by maritime war.

But we should also recognise that the Directory was responsible, either directly or indirectly, for many positive developments in the realm of the economy. For example, good harvests in 1796 and 1798, meant that the price of grain fell, thus aiding the consumer. One Director, Ramel, had a major influence. In 1797 and 1798 he achieved the first balanced budgets in French history. He also helped to reorganise the country's taxation system, making it more modern and efficient, especially in the assessment and collection of direct tax.

In important regards, the Directory predated and anticipated Napoleon. Historians now argue that, by switching from paper to metal, the 1795–99 regime helped to stabilise the currency and foster general economic confidence. Also – and perhaps even more significantly – it is claimed that the establishment of the Bank of France in 1800 was made possible by the achievements of the Directors.

The regime made its mark in other areas. For instance, in 1795 it was responsible for two developments. It founded the French Institute and also announced that:

> There is only one standard of weights and measures for the entire Republic; there shall be a platinum ruler on which will be marked the meter, which has been adopted as the fundamental unit of the whole system of measurement. Said standard

shall be executed with the greatest precision, according to the experience and observations of the commissioners responsible for the determination thereof, and it shall be deposited in the neighbourhood of the Legislative Body, as well as the *procès-verbal* of the operations which have served in determining it, so that it may be verified at all times.

The standardisation of weights and measures was a relatively minor issue, but the Directory's contribution in this area is impressive. In specific areas, the regime did operate effectively and efficiently.

But probably the biggest issue for the Directory was domestic peace. How could it be achieved? France was being undermined by counter-revolutionary uprisings. This was particularly the case in the West where the Vendée was a constant problem. It had erupted into banditry and violence in 1793 and had been an unwanted distraction throughout 1793–94. Thus, we should note the fact that General Hoche on behalf of the Directory was able to quell the Vendée in 1795–96. Peace treaties were signed and the Directors were given some breathing space.

Threats from the left and right

The crushing of the Vendée uprising was a major achievement but on its own it did not bring domestic stability. The post-Robespierre political situation was both complex and confused. The Directory pleased very few people and so it was always going to have its enemies on left and right. According to one writer, these equated to 'vile terrorism' and 'odious royalism'.

On the left there were periodic bouts of agitation. In 1798, for example, the regime was forced to act against a group of anti-Directory Jacobins. The law of 22 Floréal annulled elections in thirty departments and excluded forty-eight deputies by name (this came to be known as the Floréal coup). But the main danger came from Graccus Babeuf, who threatened the status quo in 1796. He wanted to go further than any part of the revolution had gone previously and launched a conspiracy against the regime which ended in ignominy.

But Babeuf's failure does not lessen his significance. Historians agree that his 'Conspiracy of Equals' represented an important current of thought. The main objective was an armed uprising in support of the masses against the 'bourgeois' Directory. In this vein, Babeuf stated:

2. The purpose of society is to defend … equality, often assailed by the strong and the wicked in the state of nature, and to augment the general welfare through the co-operation of all.
3. Nature has imposed upon each and every individual the obligation to work; anyone who evades his share of labour is a criminal.
4. Both work and benefits must be common to all.
5. There is oppression when one person is exhausted by labour and is destitute of everything, while another lives in luxury without doing any work at all.
6. Anyone who appropriates exclusively to himself the products of the earth or of manufacture is a criminal.
7. In a real society there ought to be neither rich nor poor.
8. The rich who are not willing to renounce their surplus in favour of the poor are enemies of the people.
9. No one, by accumulating to himself all power, may deprive another of the instruction necessary for his welfare. Education ought to be common to all.
10. The aim of the French Revolution is to destroy inequality and to re-establish the general welfare.

Babeuf went on to argue that the revolution was 'not complete'. The Constitution of 1795 was 'illegal', and only the Constitution of 1793 could bring happiness because it 'sanctioned the inalienable right of every citizen to consent to the laws, to enjoy political rights, to meet in assembly, to demand what he deems useful, to receive education, and not to die of hunger; rights which the counter-revolutionary Act of 1795 openly and totally violated'. Thus, those 'who have raised their hands against the Constitution of 1793 are guilty of common high treason'. Some historians have even argued that Babeuf's ideas were akin to a primitive form of communism.

On the right, the main threat came from resurgent royalism. On 13 Vendémiaire (5 October 1795) revolutionary troops and royalist forces confronted each other in the streets of Paris. Two years later, in 1797, the royalists were poised again after making electoral gains. According to the diaries of the Marquise de la Tour du Pin – a leading aristocrat who was forced to emigrate during the revolution – they 'had great hopes, and plots were woven in all directions. Many *émigrés* had returned. They wore rallying signs, all well-known by the police: the cape made of black velvet, a knot, I no longer remember what kind, at the corner of the handkerchief etc … And it was by these kinds of idiocies that we thought we could save France.'

By way of a retort, the Directory accused the royalists of undermining the revolution and instigated a pre-emptive strike against them which came to be known as the Fructidor coup. For the Directors, there was an underlying issue: how should they deal with 'unfavourable' election results? With significant gains for either the royalist right or the Jacobin left? The army was called on to restore order, elections were cancelled and some of the guilty royalists were arrested. Then, in an act of vengeance, the Directors enacted legislation against the relatives of *émigrés* and established military tribunals to deal with return-ing *émigrés*. The attitude of the Directory was unyielding:

> The French people have entrusted the custody of their Constitutions primarily to the fidelity of the Legislative Body

and the executive power. The integrity of such confidence has been threatened by a royalist plot, organised long since, woven with skill, and pursued with constancy. The Executive Directory has discovered the conspiracy; the guilty parties have been apprehended; the Legislative Body has promptly taken the measures which circumstances necessitated. Blood has not been shed; wisdom has governed force; valour and discipline have moderated the use thereof. National justice has been consecrated by the composure of the people. It was obvious to everyone that there was no desire to displace anything, but that there was a desire to return everything to its place.

The Directors prided themselves on their 'wisdom', on their peaceful rather than 'bloody' means. And the last line seemed to encapsulate what the regime was all about: 'returning' to the values of 1789 perhaps?

Threats from the right (and left) encouraged the regime to re-assert its republican principles. There was no question of it giving in to royalist or counter-revolutionary (or Jacobin) demands. With this in mind, the Directory stated:

Without a doubt, monarchical systems admirably suited the conspirators' aims. It was important for them to reshape the mass of the nation in the royal mould. But an indignant nation spurns them. The Republic has triumphed, and republican systems shall prove and consolidate their triumph. This shall be the sign and the fruit of victory. The republican spirit, republican ethic, and republican institutions and customs must prevail today. To embrace them, however, we must first better understand them, and this starts by defining them more precisely. The republican spirit … is composed of all that is just, equitable, good, and kind in men.

The message was clear: the Directory stood for moderate republican values.

Foreign policy: war-mongers or peace-mongers?

The coming to power of the Directors coincided with a succession of French military victories – at Lodi in May 1796, Arcola in November 1796 and Rivoli in January 1797. Moreover, by May 1797 Napoleon Bonaparte was occupying Venice. A year later, in May 1798, the French expedition to Egypt commenced and by July France had triumphed at the Battle of the Pyramids. But there were setbacks in 1799: France had to endure Austrian and Russian successes between March and July and defeat at Novi in August. On 24 August, Napoleon left Egypt and by 9 October he had returned to France. On 9 November (18 Brumaire) he installed himself in power following a *coup d'état*.

It has been almost impossible for historians to talk of the Directory and foreign policy without alluding to Bonaparte. Rudé argues that, with the coming of the Directors, 'the fate of the Republic lay less in the hands of the politicians than in those of the generals'. Cobban expands on this, claiming that the regime, 'which had welcomed the Egyptian expedition as a means of removing an ambitious and dangerous general from the scene, found that it had brought a new continental war upon itself and one which it lacked the energy or ability to cope with successfully.' It is ironic, then, that Doyle should state that in 1795, when the Directory came to power, 'The desire for peace was general after five years of battling against the whole of Europe.'

The traditional view is that in foreign policy the Directory was happy to remain at war. France had been at the centre of various conflicts since April 1792 and it is claimed that the Directors were committed to an expansionist policy and couldn't bring the war to a satisfactory close. Moreover, it is stated that the Directory was far too reliant on the army, especially after 1797. Napoleon was sent on military expeditions to Egypt and Italy; and the argument goes that these experiences, and the independence he was given, encouraged him to seize power in 1799. In effect, this is to concur with Robespierre – who had predicted early in the revolution that foreign war would inevitably lead to military dictatorship.

This view is put into even sharper focus when it is acknowledged that ordinary people were getting tired of the war. They hated conscription, felt that *la patrie* was no longer in danger (contrary to the rousing patriotic propaganda that was still emanating from the revolutionary authorities), and disliked the economic hardship that seemed to be the inevitable accompaniment to war.

The more modern interpretation is that war was a necessity. It had economic and financial benefits for France, stopped the army from interfering in domestic matters (which, given the frequency of *coup* attempts, was a blessing), and also gave the Directory a *raison d'être* and narrative. At the same time, it has been argued that the depiction of the Directory as a 'warmongering' regime is a misinformed one. In 1797, Barras and Talleyrand were involved in peace negotiations at Lille, and later in the year, in October, France signed the Treaty of Campo Formio with Austria. One key passage from this document read:

> There shall be for the future and forever a firm and inviolable peace between His Majesty the Emperor of the Romans, King of Hungary and of Bohemia, his heirs and successors, and the French Republic ... His Majesty the Emperor, King of Hungary and of Bohemia, renounces for himself and his successors, in favour of the French Republic, all his rights and titles to the former Belgic Provinces, known under the name of the Austrian Low Countries. The French Republic shall possess these countries forever, in complete sovereignty and proprietorship, and with all the territorial advantages which result therefrom.

In terms of territorial acquisitions, France benefited immensely from the treaty, taking the Austrian Netherlands, several islands in the Mediterranean, and Venetian islands in the Adriatic. It is significant that Bonaparte signed the treaty with Count Ludwig von Coblenz of Austria. He was the chief French representative at Campo Formio and it is the view of most historians that the peace treaty was an important milestone in his rise to power.

We must look for balance between the textbook and revisionist theses on the Directory. It was neither as hopeless as the traditional view suggests nor as successful as the modern view claims. The context is important. The Directors came to power in the aftermath of horrific state violence (the Terror, 1792–94) and a short period of readjustment (the Thermidorian Regime, 1794–5). So, governing France was never going to be easy. But they brought with them a set of values that were recognisable from the early years of the revolution – most notably, a belief in liberty, property, the law and capitalism.

Hindsight has also been unkind to the regime. Some histories of France have simply ignored the years 1795–99. It is as if the Directory was an interlude of little importance – it just happened to fill a gap between the violence of the Terror and the grandeur of the Bonapartist era. There was certainly no magnetic personality in the mould of a Robespierre or Napoleon to attract historians and students alike.

But the Directory had a job to do. It may have been unglamorous, but the task was an important one: to substitute stability, moderation and pragmatism for instability, extremism and dogmatism. In the circumstances, what else could a sensible set of leaders aim for? We must conclude that the Directory played a vital and perhaps understated role in returning France to normality.

The Directory came to an end with the military coup of 18 Brumaire, Year VIII, which brought Napoleon to power. It was instigated by Sieyès whose aim, via the Constitution of the Year

VIII (1799), was to stave off a Jacobin revival. But once in power, Bonaparte snubbed Sieyès and his constitutional ideas and proceeded to appoint himself First Consul and then First Consul for life. This begs the question: was Brumaire the end or the realisation of the revolution?

One view is that the Napoleonic era had little in common with the revolutionary decade. Napoleon established himself as Consul and then Emperor. His regime broke with the revolution on religion – the Concordat made peace with the Catholic Church – and also reverted to regulation in economic matters. In this sense it could be argued either that Napoleon was heir to the French monarchical tradition or that he actually symbolised a new, modern and professional approach to government. Another view sees Napoleon as a man of the revolution. After all, he was a member of the Jacobin Club and happy to do the revolutionaries' bidding in the military sphere. On coming to power he also emphasised that the gains of the revolution were secure.

But, in many respects Napoleon was unique. He was a soldier who used his military mindset to effect in the political sphere. Moreover, many of his innovations and reforms endured. It could also be argued that his authoritarian style of rule – including his use of propaganda and lack of empathy for ordinary people – had something in common with the dictators of the twentieth century.

9

Revolutionary historiography

> French historians saw themselves as crusaders for political causes
> in their own times that perpetuated the conflicts of the revolu-
> tionary period. Defending a particular point of view about the
> French Revolution was one way of legitimising the monarchy
> before 1848, or the Republic in 1848 and again after 1870, or
> the Empire from 1851 to 1870.
>
> Norman Hampson

Early writings: Burke and de Stäel

More than any other historical event perhaps, the French
Revolution has provoked and challenged historians. Sometimes
it is dangerous to attach labels to writers, but as we reflect on
two hundred years of historiography it is possible to delineate
some general positions. Liberal historians have emphasised the
progressive gains of 1789 and sought to rescue these from the
wreckage of the Terror. Conservative historians have played on
the 'extreme' and 'anarchical' nature of the revolution and
argued that, in breaking with tradition, the revolution brought
terrible consequences on France. Meanwhile, radical, left-wing
historians have upheld 1793 as a significant achievement;
moreover, those with Marxist sympathies have argued that the
revolution was fundamentally 'bourgeois' in nature. There have
also been republican and counter-revolutionary historians;

historians interested in regional perspectives on the revolution, in the ideological and philosophical background, and in interpretations 'from above' and 'from below'.

Two family lines have formed. 'The Great Tradition' denotes that group of historians who viewed the revolution as a positive, pioneering and patriotic phenomenon. It was a 'good thing', something to be lauded and upheld. But in time, another line started to emerge and enveloped all those historians who did not naturally fall within its orbit.

Edmund Burke and Madame de Staël were two of the most famous early observers of the revolution. But neither would have said that they were 'historians' in the traditional sense, or that they were actually trying to write 'history'. How could they when the dust had hardly settled on the revolution and both were 'involved', to some degree at least, in the events of the revolutionary era?

Burke's *Reflections on the Revolution in France* was written in 1790. The book was read all over Europe and as a result he gained great notoriety and fame. 'It may not be unnecessary to inform the reader,' explains Burke at the start of the book, 'that the following Reflections had their origin in a correspondence between the Author and a very young gentleman at Paris, who did him the honour of desiring his opinion upon the important transactions, which then, and ever since, have so much occupied the attention of all men.' Burke is being honest and nowhere does he imply that *Reflections* was any kind of comprehensive history.

On the whole, Burke is scathing about the revolution: 'France, by the perfidy of her leaders, has utterly disgraced the tone of lenient council in the cabinets of princes, and disarmed it of its most potent topics. She has sanctified the dark, suspicious maxims of tyrannous distrust; and taught kings to tremble at (what will hereafter be called) the delusive plausibilities of moral politicians.' He could find little in the anarchy and chaos of the period that was either admirable or impressive.

In one sense, Germaine de Staël, daughter of Necker, was an eyewitness to revolution. ('When the King came into the middle of [the] assembly to take the throne, I felt frightened for the first time. For one thing I could see that the Queen was greatly moved. She came late and the colour of her complexion was altered)'. But it could be argued that, courtesy of *Considerations on the Main Events of the French Revolution*, published posthumously in 1818, she was also its first proper historian.

Her analysis of the causes of the revolution was clear. The clergy had been inefficient, too political, and 'had lost a certain amount of public respect'. Also, the nobility, the country's 'warrior' class, had 'fallen from splendour', and the estates system in France, more generally, was riddled by 'unfair privilege'. In her writings, de Staël is preoccupied with the period 1793–94:

> Although England, like France, is stained by the murder of Charles I and the despotism of Cromwell, the Reign of Terror is a horrible and unique phenomenon … In 1793 it seemed as if France had no room for any more revolutions. Everything had already been overthrown – Crown, nobility, clergy – and the success of the Revolutionary armies made peace throughout Europe something to hope for. This is just when popular tyrannies do arise, though: as soon as the danger is past. The worst of men control themselves as long as there are obstacles and fears; after they have won, their repressed passions know no bounds.

Her natural sympathies seem to lie with the 'moderate' Girondins, for elsewhere she talks about their 'intrepid eloquence', 'their admirable presence of mind', and the fact that they were the only group of people, 'still worthy of taking their place in history'. She comes across as being slightly condescending in her attitude towards the ordinary people, with talk of 'popular tyrannies', 'the worst of men', 'repressed passions' and 'an instinct for savagery'.

Liberals and romantics

During the early years of Napoleon's rule, Louis Adolphe Thiers and François Auguste Marie Mignet studied law together in Aix-en-Provence, and also developed an interest in literature. Thereafter, their careers as writers, political activists and historians followed a similar path. Along with Armand Carrel, they founded the powerful liberal daily newspaper, *Le National*, in January 1830. As journalists, they campaigned vociferously against the restored Bourbon monarchy. It was perfectly natural for them to combine political agitation with the writing of history. Hampson states:

> The first serious historians of the Revolution were François Mignet and Adolphe Thiers, who began to publish their accounts in 1823 ... Thiers and Mignet began what was to become a Great Tradition, developed by most of their successors over the next century. They saw the Revolution as both political and social: Mignet contrasted it with the revolution in England that had merely changed the government. Thiers claimed that 1789 had put an end to a feudal constitution and a society in which the nobility had clung on to their privileges when the crown had stripped them of their political role and turned them into court pensioners.

Both men viewed the revolution as 'the inevitable product of circumstances' and also as a 'beneficent' event. This was their liberal perspective: the revolution had the potential to change the course of French history for the better.

In one sense, Thomas Carlyle was an ally of Thiers and

Mignet. He had liberal inclinations and shared many of their main concerns. But, in reality, he had little regard for their work. Carlyle's historical method was an unusual one. The general style is epic, literary and grandiose, almost Biblical in tone and, as such, in keeping with Carlyle's life as a writer and essayist. To the modern reader, *The French Revolution* reads more like a historical thriller than a piece of reflection and considered analysis. There is a helter-skelter of anecdote and vivid, colour-ful picture-painting. As Cobban puts it, 'He is the word-painter of a society in shipwreck.'

The book is based primarily on memoirs, newspaper reports, minutes of official proceedings and already-published histories of the revolution. It is highly eccentric and individualistic but it is 'history' in a way that earlier efforts probably were not or could not be. Moreover, it is 'history from below', not particularly in the sense that it focuses on the lives of the lower classes, but in the way that it tells the story of the revolution through tittle-tattle and the everyday lives of key individuals. One way to understand and explain the nature of Carlyle is to examine his commentaries on some of the key events of the revolution. On the convening of the Estates General, he writes:

> To say, let States-General be, was easy; to say in what manner they shall be, is not so easy. Since the year of 1614, there have no States-General met in France, all trace of them has vanished from the living habits of men. Their structure, powers, methods of procedure, which were never in any measure fixed, have now become wholly a vague possibility. Clay which the potter may shape, this way or that: – say rather, the twenty-five millions of potters; for so many have now, more or less, a vote in it! How to shape the States-General? There is a problem. Each Body-corporate, each privileged, each organised Class has secret hopes of its own in that matter; and also secret misgivings of its own, – for, behold, this monstrous twenty-million Class,

hitherto the dumb sheep which these others had to agree about the manner of shearing, is now also arising with hopes! It has ceased or is ceasing to be dumb; it speaks through Pamphlets, or at least brays and growls behind them, in unison, – increasing wonderfully their volume of sound.

Along with Adolph Thiers, François Guizot is probably the best example of the historian-politician or politician-historian. Of course, in nineteenth-century France there was a significant overlap between the two professions. Guizot stands out as one of the foremost romantic-idealist historians, and also one of the key political figures of the period. He had a long and distinguished political career, which culminated in his role as King Louis Philippe's first minister during the Orleanist era.

Guizot was born two years prior to the Fall of the Bastille. He studied in Switzerland and moved on to a legal career in Paris. Thereafter he turned his attention to literary matters and his arrival as a historian came in 1812 when he was appointed professor of modern history at the Sorbonne. Elected as a *député* in 1830, he served Louis Philippe as minister of the interior and public instruction (1832–37), and started to dominate government in the early- and mid-1840s. He was appointed premier in 1847 but was ousted by the revolutionaries of 1848.

The general historical consensus is that Guizot moved more and more to the right as the 1830s and 1840s progressed, coming to personify the selfish, narrow-minded philosophy of Orleanism. From the start he openly paraded his ideology. In a speech of 5 October 1831 he declared:

I have heard equality much spoken of; we have called it the fundamental principle of our political organisation. I am afraid there has been a great mistake. Without doubt there are universal rights, equal rights for all, rights inherent in humanity and which no human being can be stripped of without injustice and

> disorder ... But will political rights be of this order? It is
> through tradition, through heredity that families, peoples, and
> history subsist; without tradition, without heredity you would
> have nothing of that. It is through the personal activity of
> families, peoples, and individuals that produces the perfectibil-
> ity of the human race. Suppress it, and you will cause the
> human race to fall to the rank of the animals.

As regards his view of history, and by implication his view of the
revolution, there are mixed signals: the trust in 'aristocracy' and
'tradition', but also the emphasis on 'rights'.

Jules Michelet's *History of the French Revolution*, published
between 1847 and 1853, is a wonderful book to read because
the author is so open and disarming in his prejudices, both
positive and negative. As Hampson put it:

> With Michelet the Great Tradition found its most eloquent and
> extreme spokesman. To present the bare outline of his
> argument is like paraphrasing one of Shakespeare's tragedies:
> one can convey a general impression of what it was all about
> but the real meaning is inseparable from the hypnotic language
> that is an essential part of it.

When Michelet wrote his history, there was still a little naivety
about what the job of the historian entailed. Thus, when he talks
about his technique as a historian, he reveals that he establishes
and verifies his findings, 'either by written testimony, or by such
as I have gathered from the lips of old men'.

Michelet is unfailingly honest in the way he says the revolution – studying and writing about it – affected him. He sees it as
a personal joy to be able to recount such a heroic period:

> I am endeavouring to describe to-day that epoch of unanimity,
> that holy period, when a whole nation, free from all party
> distinction, as yet a comparative stranger to the opposition of
> classes, marched together under a flag of brotherly love ...

These are the sacred days of the world – thrice happy days for history. For my part, I have had my reward, in the mere narration of them. Never, since the composition of my Maid of Orleans, have I received such a ray from above, such a vivid inspiration from Heaven.

From de Tocqueville to Marxist orthodoxy

Where does Alexis de Tocqueville fit in? He was an 'anxious aristocrat', according to Palmer, one who felt that democracy was inevitable but dangerous. It is possible to make a connection between de Tocqueville and the liberal historians of the early nineteenth century. He shared many of their instincts and inclinations and, undeniably, placed a premium on the protection of liberty.

De Tocqueville's major work was *The Old Regime and the French Revolution* (1856). It is important to understand that he was writing in a particular kind of climate. 'The Springtime of the Peoples' – the name given to the kaleidoscope of liberal-nationalist revolutions in 1848 – had a distinctly French flavour, for the initial revolutionary moment had taken place in Paris. For de Tocqueville, the revolution of 1848 was an interesting and curious political event. To some extent, he admired the working-class Parisian agitators who were at the forefront of the uprising. They had risked their lives for a principle they believed in, and de Tocqueville, albeit in a somewhat detached and patronising manner, could respect this. But, as an aristocrat, he knew that 1848 was fundamentally 'bad', and he knew he could not, or should not, sympathise with its objectives.

The revolution could not but impact upon de Tocqueville's writings. It had the effect of frightening the middle and upper classes, and as a liberal aristocrat – and someone who was actually present in Paris during the disturbances – he was certainly not immune from feelings of fear and unease. 'It was ... no laughing matter but something sinister and frightening to see the state of Paris when I returned there,' he wrote.

> In that city there were a hundred thousand armed workmen formed into regiments, without work and dying of hunger, but with heads full of vain theories and chimerical hopes. Society was cut in two: those who had nothing united in common envy; those who had anything united in common terror. There were no longer ties of sympathy linking these two great classes, and a struggle was everywhere assumed to be inevitable soon. There had already been physical clashes with different results between the bourgeois and the people – for these old names had been revived as battle cries – at Limoges and at Rouen. In Paris hardly a day passed without some attack or threat to the propertied classes' capital or income.

Given these feelings, it was inevitable that de Tocqueville's attitude to 1848 would come to colour his view of 1789.

Against the backdrop of a new, progressive regime – the Third Republic – historians came to re-evaluate the revolution, often in quite political and ideological terms. It is also important to note that the centenary of the revolution was celebrated during this period, a significant landmark that gave rise to an increase in historiographical writings. Here the two most notable names were Hippolyte Taine and Alphonse Aulard.

Taine offered a sociological interpretation of events that, in time, marked him out as the archetypal conservative onlooker. He had little positive to say about the Jacobins:

> Aside from the great mass of well-disposed people fond of a quiet life, the Revolution has sifted out and separated from the rest all who are fanatical, brutal or perverse enough to have lost respect for others; these form the new garrison – sectarians

blinded by their creed, the roughs (*assommeurs*) who are hardened by their calling, and those who make all they can out of their offices. None of this class are scrupulous concerning human life or property; for, as we have seen, they have shaped the theory to suit themselves, and reduced popular sovereignty to their sovereignty.

Neither does Taine hide his emotions. He implies that the Jacobins are dirty and also corrupt and self-seeking.

Aulard was the first professional historian of the French Revolution, and he devoted his life to this study. A professor at the University of Paris, he founded the Société de l'Histoire de la Révolution and the bi-monthly review *Révolution Française*. Instead of monarchy, Aulard favoured a brand of democratic republicanism that was very much in vogue with the establishment of the Third Republic.

Essentially, Aulard regarded the conservative interpretation of Taine as subjective, and so, as a corrective, he developed what was, to all intents and purposes, a republican and anti-clerical view of the revolution. This is an illuminating example of the way in which historians have 'confronted' each other over the meaning of the revolution. Aulard's interpretation of the revolutionary decade is political rather than socio-economic in emphasis. And he makes no bones about this:

The economic and social history of the Revolution is dispersed over so many sources that it is actually impossible in one lifetime to deal with them all, or even with the most important. He who would write this history unaided could only here and there attain the whole truth, and would end by producing only a superficial sketch of the whole, drawn at second or third hand. But in the case of political history, if it be reduced to the facts I have chosen, it is possible for a man, in the course of twenty years, to read the laws of the Revolution, the principal journals, correspondences, deliberations, speeches, election papers, and the biographies of those who played a part in the political life of the time.

In the early and middle decades of the twentieth century, the 'Great Tradition' of revolutionary historiography was dominated by a group of leftist writers including Jean Jaurès, Albert Mathiez, Georges Lefebvre and Albert Soboul. The way in which they delineated a 'bourgeois revolution' occurring in 1790s France was a defining moment in the history of revolutionary studies. What is more, they put their case in such a convincing manner that the Marxist interpretation of the revolution gradually came to be regarded as the orthodoxy.

The key landmarks in French Marxist historiography were: 1898 – Jean Jaurès, *Histoire Socialiste de la Révolution française*; 1927 – Albert Mathiez, *The French Revolution*; 1939 – George Lefebvre, *Quatre Vingt Neuf*; and 1965 – Albert Soboul, *A Short History of the French Revolution*. The writers who put forward the Marxist line on the revolution began to coalesce under the banner of the 'Annales School'. It was also interesting that many of the key left-wing historians were not just historians but political activists too, involved in the French socialist or communist parties.

In chapter 2 we considered the Marxist interpretation of the revolution and, in particular, its origins. Now we must place the emergence of left-wing theories in context. For Marx himself, 1789 was an important reference point. He refers to it often in his writings, and talks about it as the 'old' and 'great' revolution as if in veneration. He was curious about the whole revolutionary tradition in France, and also, for partisan reasons, concerned, if not obsessed, about 'revolution' as an idea.

The main question was this: to what extent was the revolution of 1789 a 'bourgeois revolution'? In other words, did the experience of France in the period 1789–99 conform to Marx's delineation of the key 'scientific' stages in history? And, looking back on the revolution, could the experience of France be made, or forced, to fit in with Marx's model? It was with these fundamental issues that Marxist and left-leaning historians were made to grapple. The point to be made is this: although, to a large extent, the research of Marxist historians was driven by ideology, there is no doubt that their ideas gained wide currency and acceptance.

Revisionism: 'soft' and 'hard'

'Soft revisionism' is the term coined to describe the efforts of a range of post-war historians to discredit the Marxist orthodoxy. Led by Alfred Cobban, these writers continued to place the emphasis on social and economic history; but, they had serious concerns about the narrowness and 'scientific' nature of the Marxist line.

Most commentators are agreed that the 'chief protagonist' or 'father of revisionism' is Cobban, whose most important work was *The Social Interpretation of the French Revolution* (1964). At the time, this book was slightly neglected, but it gradually acquired the reputation of a path-breaking work. On one level it was a critique of the Marxist standpoint. On another it was a 'non-Marxist social interpretation'. It still placed the emphasis on social and economic factors, but it veered away from any kind of deterministic approach.

Other independent-minded, non-Marxist revisionists buttressed the Cobban position. In the words of Kates, these writers were 'not known for their political activism or political labels'. It could be argued that whereas Marxist historians had a general approach to uphold, this new breed of writers came to the subject without any obvious prejudices to propogate. Most notable in this context were G.V. Taylor, 'Non-capitalist wealth and the origins of the French Revolution', *American History Review* (1967); Norman Hampson, *A Social History of the French Revolution* (1963); and J.M. Thompson, *The French Revolution* (1966). Taylor's was a particularly important contribution, as he, like Cobban, argued for an overlap between the bourgeoisie and the aristocracy as classes. It is relevant to point out that Cobban was English and Taylor was American, for, very gradually, a shift in power was taking place – with French Marxist historians being usurped by Anglo-Saxon revisionists.

'Soft revisionism' was based on a number of key tenets. First, Cobban and his co-accusers objected to the pseudo-scientific nature of Marxist theory. It seemed that Marxist interpretations were determined to put theory first and facts second; the revisionists placed a premium on the facts above all else. Second, this wave of revisionists had serious reservations about the main claims of Lefebvre and his Marxist allies regarding the nature of the aristocracy and bourgeoisie – that is, if they were distinct classes. In short, they argued that the aristocracy was not 'feudal', the bourgeoisie was neither 'united' nor 'capitalist', and it was the peasantry, rather than the middle-class bourgeoisie, who were responsible for the overthrow of the *Ancien Régime*. Third, the revisionists could not hide the fact that, ultimately, they were actually questioning, and perhaps even downplaying, the significance of the revolution and 1789 as a watershed (although Cobban, for one, refuted this: 'It must not be supposed, though Georges Lefebvre did, that I am trying to deny the existence of the French Revolution; I merely want to discover what it was').

'Hard revisionism' went even further. It claimed not only that the Marxist interpretation was misinformed, but also that any theory of the revolution based on social factors was inherently faulty. As such, 'hard revisionists' put the emphasis on political factors, and other factors less easy to categorise. They ensured that the work of Cobban, Taylor and others was not simply regarded as a 'blip'. They consolidated, but also enhanced, the revisionist offensive.

The central figure in 'hard revisionism' has been François Furet, whose ideas on the revolution cannot be separated from his own personal background. He was an ex-Marxist and wrote much of his history in the 1970s, 1980s and 1990s, as the fortunes of the French Communist Party entered into almost terminal decline and became something of an irrelevance in modern French politics. In *Interpreting the French Revolution*, he was aware of this context:

> I am writing these lines in the spring of 1977, at a time when the criticism of Soviet totalitarianism, and more generally of all power claiming its source in Marxism, is no longer the monopoly, or near monopoly, of right-wing thought and has become a central theme in the reflections of the Left. What is important here, in referring to the historically related entities of Right and Left, is not that the criticism from the Left, which has occupied a culturally dominant position in France since the end of the Second World War, carries more weight than criticism from the Right. Much more important is that in indicting the USSR or China the Right has no need to adjust any part of its heritage and can simply stay within the bounds of counter-revolutionary thought. The Left, on the other hand, must face up to facts that compromise its beliefs, which are as old as those of the Right.

This background explains to a large extent Furet's derogatory attitude towards Marxist historians of the revolution.

It would be difficult to disagree with the view which says that the French Revolution is one of the most *complex*, and also one of the most *analysed*, historical events. Cobban says that, over the decades, interpretations have tended to fall into two main categories – either 'conspiracy' or 'destiny'. Those hostile to the revolution do tend to view it as some kind of 'plot' or 'punishment' meted out on France, whereas those more favourable can sometimes get carried away by the inevitability and wonder of 1789.

But the real question is this: why has the revolution provoked so many widely differing interpretations? There are a number of angles we could take on this issue. First, the rich tapestry of revolutionary historiography reflects, and almost imitates, the kaleidoscopic nature of France's history of revolutions. Over the last two centuries the French political landscape has been ever-changing. There have been absolute monarchies, constitutional monarchies, republics and empires – and this has meant that, on occasions, historians, attached to a specific regime, have considered the period 1789–99 from a partisan point of view, with the intention of scoring political points. Thus, we have to treat the views of historians with more caution and scepticism than perhaps is usual.

Second, there is the event itself. In essence, the 'revolution' comprised three 'mini-revolutions': the liberal revolt (1789–91), the illiberal interlude (1792–94), and the reversion to moderation (1794–99). So, when historians come to examine the event, they can either become fascinated by its evolving trajectory or blinkered by one particular phase with which they seek to identify themselves. Either way, there is a compulsion to discover more.

10

The French Revolution today

WINNER SARKOZY PROMISES A FRENCH REVOLUTION

France is on course for a Right-wing revolution after Nicolas Sarkozy secured an emphatic victory over his Socialist rival, Ségolène Royal, last night to become the country's next president.

Henry Samuel and Harry de Quetteville in Paris,
Daily Telegraph, 7 May 2007

A revolution that is everywhere

For journalists and sub-editors across the world, the revolution has been a god-send. Any major news story or radical development in France? Just insert the phrase 'French Revolution' and the headline almost writes itself. So, in recent times, we have had: 'FRANCE PLANS REVOLUTION IN SPACE', 'SARKOZY SET TO UNLEASH NEW FRENCH REVOLUTION', 'A NEW FRENCH REVOLUTION'S CREED: LET THEM RIDE BIKES', 'THE NEXT FRENCH REVOLUTION: NICOLAS SARKOZY SETS OUT HIS PLANS FOR A GREEN FUTURE' and many, many more.

There is a serious point here. The French Revolution is such a well-known historical event that headline-writers know that people will immediately understand and connect with references to it. What other two-word phrase could do the same? Have other landmark events – such as the English Civil War or the Reformation, say – had such an afterlife in the public consciousness? The answer is probably in the negative. So the phrase, and thus, we must assume, the event itself, still has currency in the twenty-first century.

There are other indicators of the revolution's legacy. It is an oft-quoted tale but when, in the middle of the twentieth century, Chinese revolutionary leader Zhou Enlai was asked about the significance of the revolution, he replied: 'It's too early to say.' This is a hackneyed story, but it reveals an essential truth. In many contexts, the significance and legacy of the revolution has been immeasurable.

Likewise, on a recent trip to Paris I met up with a group of French friends. We sat down for dinner and started chatting. I was expecting a conversation about football or music, but instead one guest said to another: 'Jean, let me ask you a hypothetical question: If we were transported back in time two hundred years, and you were alive in Paris during the 1790s, which political grouping would you have been loyal to? Would you have been a Girondin or Jacobin? A Feuillant or Hébertist?' I was astonished, and also fascinated, by what I was hearing. In contemporary France, the revolution is still a live topic for debate, even among young twenty-somethings who only had personal experience of the modern Fifth Republic. Amazing!

In chapter 9 we saw how historians have maintained an interest in the events of 1789–99. Here we will focus on the way that politicians in modern-day France still use the revolution as a key point of reference in their discourse. Why is this? And how do 'ordinary people' feel about the event, more than two centuries on? Key themes will be anniversaries and commemorations, right- and left-wing views of the revolution today, political language and vocabulary, and the significance of the 'rights of man' as a contemporary issue. In his book, *After the French Revolution*, Jack Hayward talks about the revolution's 'unfinished agenda' and this idea will underpin much of the discussion in this chapter.

The best place to start is the centre of Paris. The revolutionary events of 1789–99 took place almost exclusively in the capital city; and twenty-first century visitors are reminded of this almost constantly. Take a wander and you encounter, among other things, the Tuileries Gardens and the Place de la Bastille.

As arguably the most famous landmark of the revolution, the Bastille receives its fair share of attention. 'What remains today of the fortress?' asks a tourism website.

> Aside from the pavement reminders ... you can see the base of the fortress's ironically named Liberté tower at the Square Henri Galli, [and] a mini public garden where Boulevard Henri IV meets the Pont de Sully ... There are commemorative plaques on the walls of 3 Place de la Bastille and 5 rue St. Antoine. And if you enter the Bastille Métro station and go to the platform of the Pantin line, you can see some of the ancient masonry.

Go to another website and the view is slightly less positive: 'You may have a romantic idea about the Bastille, based on movies and books and so you may want to see this famous place during your stay in Paris. Being there where the French Revolution began on July 14, 1789, where the poor stood up against oppression by royal absolutism. Bah! Dream on, but don't go there – you would be very disappointed!'

The revolution has also gone underground. The Paris Métro – the capital's network of subterranean trains – is keen to educate both residents and tourists. You can take a train from stations with a variety of revolutionary-era names, including Voltaire, République, Convention, Assemblée Nationale and Campo Formio. And that's not to mention Nation and Liberté – abstract outcomes of the revolution that have been transformed into station names – and many other phrases and place names with revolutionary connotations.

Anniversaries and commemorations

In the early years of the twenty-first century, Bastille Day is as significant as ever. Not only is it a public holiday but the tradition is that festivities are staged across the country. The authorities describe it as 'a republican feast combined with a recreational fête'. In Paris a huge parade is held on the Champs-Élysées, with the President of the Republic and millions of TV viewers looking on. The French armed forces are present and in recent years an invitation has also gone out to military units from France's allies. In 2004, the centenary of the Entente Cordiale, Britain sent personnel from the Royal Marines, Household Cavalry Mounted Regiment, Grenadier Guards and King's Troop, Royal Horse Artillery to join the celebration. The USA and the EU have also been represented at recent parades.

There are other aspects to modern Bastille Day celebrations. The President usually holds a special garden party at the Palais de l'Elysée and gives a major interview to the French press. In theory, the President has the right – via Article 17 of the French Constitution – to pardon petty offenders; and between 1991 and 2007 the incumbents did choose to exercise this prerogative. And Bastille Day also has special resonance for cyclists in the Tour de France. It usually falls during the race – and French riders normally make a mad dash to be stage winners on that day!

Bastille Day became a military festival under the Directory, was virtually ignored by Napoleon, but came back to prominence under the Third Republic. It officially became France's national day in 1880 and municipalities were encouraged to erect statues, hold functions and ceremonies in schools, distribute gifts to local people and also engage in bell-ringing and flag-flying. As the French authorities have put it:

The main function of the national day, which established a new symbol, Marianne, a personification of the Republic, was to ensure national cohesion and to re-establish France's military power based on the collective memory. Busts of Marianne were inaugurated in public places and citizens could buy lithographs of her in shops, showing her wearing the Phrygian cap (a symbol of the freedom conquered by the people) and draped in the tricolour or surrounded by a cluster of flags (a symbol of the triumphant nation).

In Paris, Bastille Day festivities were initially held at Longchamp but in 1918 they were switched to the Champs-Élysées where a massive victory parade ('*défilé de la victoire*') led by the triumphant marshals, Joffre, Foch and Pétain, was staged. For obvious reasons, no celebrations were allowed in Paris during the German occupation of France (1940–44) but, in a gesture of defiance and resistance, a company of the commando Kieffer, of the Forces Navales Françaises Libres, did parade through the streets of London. In 1971 women were involved in the parade for the first time and between 1974 and 1981 President Valéry Giscard d'Estaing altered the route of the parade in an attempt to commemorate key events during the revolution.

Quatorze Julliet is now celebrated around the world. Type the words 'Bastille Day' into an internet search engine and you are made aware of thousands of special events that have been held or are scheduled for future years. In the USA, for example, there were celebrations in all the major towns and cities in 2008. In Seattle, Le Bal des Pompiers, Le Bistrot and La Scene ('on our two stages, l'Olympia and l'Elysée Montmartre, local and French bands will have you stomping your feet and rocking your body. *Faîtes entrer les artistes!*'). Likewise, in Los Angeles,

The Bastille Day festival promotes French heritage and culture and celebrates the undying ties between French and American citizens ... This year for the first time, West Hollywood, a young, and vibrant community with a colourful and entertaining past will host the Bastille Day Festival 2008. In its seventh year, this event promises to be one of the city's best cultural events, with all-day festivities, spectacular live entertainment, international music, dance, food and wine from France.

Since 1880, Bastille Day may have had its critics – those on the conservative right who have not appreciated its secular and republican associations – but it remains a key part of the revolution's legacy.

Political language and symbols

In 2005, as President Jacques Chirac was campaigning for a 'Yes' vote on the EU constitution, the BBC reported:

Rather than promoting a neo-liberal economic framework, as some voters fear, the constitution would enshrine French values, Mr Chirac insisted ... Responding to questions from two French journalists, Mr Chirac denied that the EU constitution would destroy the French social model and replace it with an Anglo-Saxon style economy. On the contrary, he said, the treaty was 'essentially of French inspiration' – it was 'the best possible' choice for France. He called the text the 'daughter of 1989', the year the Berlin Wall fell, and 'especially the daughter of 1789', referring to the French Revolution. It would only increase French and German influence in Europe, ensuring that the two founding nations had a decisive say in the new, enlarged EU of twenty-five, he said.

What we see here is the President of France invoking the memory of the French Revolution for political effect. Away from the actual debate about the European constitution, what is significant is Chirac's strategy. People had nothing to fear, he was arguing, because the document in question was 'related' to both 1989 and 1789 in terms of its origins, content and rationale.

In a similar way, the French flag has come to have symbolic value. The 'modern' *tricolore* was adopted during the revolution, in 1794: blue and red were the traditional colours of Paris, while white connoted the Kingdom of France. Thereafter, even though it became the national flag quite late on in the revolution (after the liberal and illiberal phases), the *tricolore* came to be associated with ideas of freedom and liberation. As such, throughout the nineteenth and twentieth centuries, *tricolore* flags – of different colours – were adopted by a number of countries who wished to proclaim their liberty and independence, including Belgium, Ireland, Italy, Romania and many others.

In France the symbolism inherent in the red–white–and–blue *tricolore* is evidenced by the fact that later regimes or administrations of a royalist hue actually dispensed with the flag. This happened under the restored Bourbon kings (1814–30), who preferred a white flag, and at the time of the monarchist fightback during the Third Republic, when the Bourbon pretender, the Comte de Chambord, said that he would only take the throne if the *tricolore* was replaced, again, by the white flag. The quasi-monarchist Vichy regime also had problems with the *tricolore*. It detested the Third Republic – which had fallen in 1940 – and was determined to 'make a new start'. So, in terms of words, it substituted 'The French State' for 'Republic', and as regards the national flag it instituted a new version of the *tricolore* – defaced with fasces and stars (traditional Roman symbols that European fascist and semi-fascist movements had updated and taken as their own).

By contrast, regimes and movements that wanted to parade their progressive nature could do so by utilising the *tricolore*. This happened in 1830 when the Orleanist regime headed by Louis Philippe came to power. Louis was a monarch who tried to appeal to both royalists and revolutionaries and in an effort to emphasise his modernity, and his determination not to be as error-prone as the Bourbons, he reinstated the *tricolore* as the French flag. A century later, General Charles de Gaulle, leader of the French Resistance, made a similar gesture. His Free French forces used a *tricolore* defaced with a red Cross of Lorraine as their flag. Even Jean-Marie Le Pen, leader of the far-right Front National today, ultilises the *tricolore* for political purposes. As a man of the right, he condemns the revolution unreservedly, but this has not discouraged his party from exploiting the French flag for political purposes. Almost every piece of FN literature and merchandise is emblazoned with the colours red, white and blue; and the party has even instituted its own 'patriotic' festival, La Fête Bleu-Blanc-Rouge. Of course, Le Pen does not see the supreme irony in all of this.

The legacy of the revolution was also brought into focus by the Bicentenary of 1989. Some commentators predicted that the 200th anniversary celebrations would be a damp squib. For example, the historian François Furet declared that the French Revolution 'was over,' and the editor of *Le Monde*, Andre Fontaine, was quoted as saying, 'Two or three years ago I was among those who thought that the bicentennial would reopen old wounds. But so many of our quarrels have been settled – colonialism, the role of the school, the place of the church.' But, in a sense, both men underestimated the power and symbolism inherent in the revolution.

President François Mitterrand was the key. In 1989 he masterminded a huge and grandiose celebration and used the opportunity of the Bicentenary to shape policy in various areas. In international affairs he tried to lead from the front. On 11 July 1989, the Paris correspondent of the *New York Times* put it like this:

As the leaders of the seven leading industrialised democracies prepare to meet here on Friday, President François Mitterrand of France is pushing for the annual Group of Seven summit conference to focus on helping the world's poor nations. With France celebrating the 200th anniversary of its Revolution, Mr Mitterrand wants the talks to help lighten the third world's $1.3 trillion debt burden ... While some French politicians and newspapers have accused President Mitterrand of trying to turn the 'bicentennial' summit meeting into a coronation, Mr Mitterrand's aides say his goal for the talks is to carry on the ideals of the French Revolution.

He also had significant architectural ambitions. For the *Independent*:

Mitterrand's *grands projets* have, without doubt, enhanced the face of Paris. Ambitious, bold and expensive, they include the Musee d'Orsay ... the Louvre pyramid and the same museum's magnificent Richelieu Wing de Rivoli ... The *grands projets* were only the most radical part of the facelift Paris underwent in time to face the bicentenary of the Revolution in 1989. Gates and domes throughout the heart of the city were adorned with glistening new coats of gold leaf. Today, the old centre of Paris is a daunting and magnificent thing.

But, not everyone shared Mitterrand's rose-tinted view of the revolution. In the West of France many local people were upset that the Bicentenary seemed to ignore the 'genocide' that the revolutionary authorities had perpetrated on the Vendée. It was as if the 'crimes' of the revolution had been air-brushed out of history. One newspaper carried the story of Baron Armel de Wismes, a noble and historian who wears a black tie of mourning each year on the anniversary of Louis XVI's execution. He was quoted as saying: 'In France, someone may pass indifferently by a place where his grandfather was executed. But people do not walk indifferently past a piece of land that was taken from their family.' This seemed to sum up the attitude of the Vendéans.

In an article published in 1996, Sophie Masson focused on the legacy of the revolt. She highlighted the attitude of modern Vendéans:

> The atrocities multiplied, the exterminations systematic and initiated from the very top, and carried out with glee at the bottom. At least 300,000 people were massacred during that time, and those of the intruders who refused to do the job were either shot or discredited utterly. But still the people resisted ... That was two hundred years ago; but at the recent bicentenary celebrated by the intruders, not a mention was made of the dead. Not a mention was made of the genocide. It was the people themselves who remembered. For that is what the intruders did not take into account: memory. The people still tell the tale, vividly, with pain. Many people in Vendée who keep the memory in their hearts refuse to vote at all in general elections, considering that the soul of the republic itself is soiled and flawed. They find it bitter indeed that the 1989 bicentenary ignored them completely. There are some who would sanctify all the Chouans, would make of them impossibly perfect heroes.

It was no real surprise, therefore, when Philippe de Villiers, the conservative president of the Vendée regional council, emerged on the national political scene. He published a controversial pamphlet entitled *Open Letter to the Choppers of Heads and Liars of the Bicentenary* and gained significant media exposure. At the time of Bicentenary, he stated: 'For two centuries, people have been made to be ashamed to be from the Vendée, but the truth is that all the great terrorists of the twentieth century have taken Robespierre as their model.'

The view that began to take hold in 1989 was that France had become 'smug' and 'self-satisfied'. In the West of France, Alix le Cadre, deputy mayor of Savenay, claimed that local residents could still be divided into royalist 'whites' and republican 'blues'. Her argument was that the Bicentenary celebrations were shallow and superficial: 'It is a lot easier to dress up schoolchildren in eighteenth century costumes and have them march around than to look into things in depth. No one wants to scratch below the surface.' On a national level, this view was echoed by social critic Jean Baudrillard: 'This is a country that lives too much from commemorations and from a patrimony of symbolic inheritances. Now it is in the process of congratulating itself about the Revolution. The French live in cultural incest.'

The 'rights of man' as a political issue

As we have seen, a milestone in the revolution was the *Declaration of the Rights of Man*, approved by the National Assembly on 26 August 1789. This became a landmark document – an albeit hasty attempt on behalf of the middle-class instigators of the revolution to outline what it stood for. Although the revolution moved on and the *Declaration* came to be viewed as an imperfect document, it retained its significance.

In the decades that followed, the 'rights of man' became a key debating point. The revolutions of the 1830s and 1848 were fought out over notions of liberty and equality, and thereafter every experiment in republicanism (the First Republic 1792–1802, the Second 1848–52, the Third 1875–1940, the Fourth 1944–58, and the Fifth 1958–) would honour and celebrate the rights of man.

In the last thirty years, with the French political spectrum as polarised as ever, the rights of man have become a major issue for parties of the left and right. The crucial date was 1981, when the socialist Mitterrand became president. After decades of right-wing and centrist rule, this was a major departure – and came to be known as '*l'alternance*'.

Mitterrand's left-wing administration put forward a radical and progressive vision. The President himself made regular references to the *Declaration* and the rights of man in his statements and speeches. He gained a reputation as a champion of human rights worldwide and even commissioned a new building, the Monument to the Rights of Man and the Citizen, in the shadow of the Eiffel Tower. In 1988, at the height of the Mitterrand era, Thomas Bishop of New York University offered some perspective on the issue: 'The revolution was a world historical event as opposed to just a French event. It seems to me that the Rights of Man is the part of the heritage of the French Revolution that is getting more play in this country and more play in France, than any other part. Nothing has emerged from the French Revolution that was more important than that.'

At around the same time – and, according to some observers, not unconnected to the rise of the left – the far right was on the rise. The Front National, led by Jean-Marie Le Pen, had been formed in 1972. Its breakthrough came in 1983 and by the late 1980s it was polling ten to fifteen per cent in parliamentary and presidential elections. The FN believes in a 'closed' and 'defensive' nation, with rights and benefits allocated according to a policy of 'national preference'. This is obviously controversial in itself, but the FN has also contrasted its philosophy with that of the left. It is here that they have characterised, and perhaps even caricatured, the socialist position. For party leaders, any policy that isn't based on hardline nationalism is suspect. They realise that the left is much more positive about immigration and multiculturalism, and that modern-day socialists are keen to honour the legacy of 1789 and the rights of man. And so, Le Pen and his colleagues made a conscious decision to demonise the Socialist Party on account of its identification with the revolution.

Twenty years on, the FN position has not altered a great deal. The party still believes in a hierarchy of rights and differentiating them according to nationality. Le Pen has recently argued: 'There are the rights of man, there could be the rights of Europeans and there are the rights of nationals. One does not exclude the other ... There can't be social solidarity except within the national framework.' His would-be successor, his daughter Marine, is equally forthright and, it should be said, vague:

National identity is a feeling, it's like love, and can you define love? Being French is the consciousness of belonging to a people who have a common history, a common territory, a common future and above all a common language. It goes far beyond simple regulations. *La nationalité française soit s'hérite soit se mérite* [French nationality has to be either inherited or deserved]. The last homeless French person must have greater rights than any foreigner, however talented, clever or respectful the foreigner may be. Because that French person's father may have been a *paysan*, his grandfather maybe died at Verdun. He is the heir to all who have built France.

On the right it isn't just Le Pen and the FN who have attacked the Socialists' position. In 1989 – the year of the Bicentenary – Philippe de Villiers mocked the hypocrisy of Mitterrand and his government. How could they talk about 'human rights' and the 'rights of man' when the revolutionary government was responsible for 'genocide' in the Vendée? 'I have read all of the official bicentennial literature and it is incredible that there is no mention of the Terror. The first right of man is the right to truth,' said de Villiers. He went on to claim that the right, in the guise of the Vendée rebels, rather than the left were the true defenders of the rights of man.

In the popular imagination, France is a country of revolutions, political extremes and direct-action tactics. The man in the street would draw a straight line between the Storming of the Bastille in the eighteenth century and the violent industrial disputes that have involved farmers, lorry drivers and postal workers in more recent times. But, in reality, the legacy of the revolution is more subtle than that. Over the past two centuries, liberal and illiberal interpretations of 1789 have been competing for space. Should we glorify the rights of man or remind ourselves that terror and totalitarianism were an intrinsic part of the revolution? The truth is that politicians, whether of today, tomorrow or yesterday, cannot ignore the revolution and its after-effects.

Epilogue

It is perhaps inevitable that any history of the French Revolution should be, up to a point, a commemoration. It can be a royalist commemoration, where one weeps over the misfortunes of the king and lost legitimacy. We have also seen 'bourgeois' commemorations, which celebrate the founding of a national contract. Or it can be a revolutionary commemoration, which emphasises the dynamism of the founding event and its promises for the future.

François Furet

So what has this concise history of the French Revolution proved? What have we discovered and learnt? Where do we go from here? The backdrop to the revolution is not simply the period 1787–89. It is centuries of Old Regime rule: the absolutism of kings, the dominance of the Church and the aristocracy, and the importance attached to feudal relationships and tradition.

The story proceeds from the Aristocratic Reaction through to the *cahiers* and the calling of the Estates General. The epic narrative of 1789 centres on the Tennis Court Oath, the Fall of the Bastille, the 'Great Fear' and the publication of the first key document of the revolution, the *Declaration of the Rights of Man*. The revolution settles down in the period 1790–92 but there are still important questions to be answered: How much power should the King retain, if any? To what extent will the revolution, and the revolutionaries, remain united? How will the new regime deal with the Church?

By the autumn of 1792, with the country at war and the infrastructure of the Terror in place, all these questions have been answered: the monarchy has been abolished, the revolutionary coalition has fractured into Girondins and Jacobins, and the latter – soon to gain complete control of the state – have plans in place to eradicate the influence of Catholicism. Thenceforth, the revolution is at its most radical, but also in its most vulnerable state. With an ongoing war to manage, and a range of counter-revolutionary forces to contend with, the Jacobins could not offer the stability that the country required. But the two post-Terror regimes – Thermidor and the Directory – were able to consolidate and return the country to moderation and policies that were reminiscent of those put forward in the early part of the revolution.

Beyond the narrative, there are important issues at stake. This interpretation of the period 1789–99 has placed the emphasis on a range of themes. Essentially, the revolution was about political ideologies. It was a battleground with liberal, conservative and (in 1793–94) early socialist ideas competing for influence. At the same time, the forces of radicalism came into conflict with those of reaction. Was the ideal system of government an absolute monarchy, a constitutional monarchy or a republic?

Alternatively, 1789 can be viewed through the lens of class and economics. Left-wing writers may have gone too far in their depiction of a 'bourgeois revolution' (it was surely not as simple as that) but it is important to recognise that a process of change was impacting on French society. The First and Second estates were desperate to maintain their influence, and those at the top of the Third Estate felt that their talents were being ignored. At the same time, ordinary people were finding a voice, on the streets, in clubs and societies, and in the 'crowd'.

For these and other reasons it could be argued that the revolution was a milestone in European history. A new language and a new set of political players emerged. In 1789, the

Declaration of the Rights of Man talked of liberty and (limited) equality; by contrast, in 1793–94, the policies of the Jacobin government were characteristic of an embryonic totalitarianism. Historians of the revolution have also played their part. They have analysed and reanalysed the sources and in recent years have grappled with interesting issues such as gender, economics, regionalism, culture and society.

What can be said with certainty is that interest in the revolution shows little sign of abating.

Chronology

1787

22 February:	Meeting of first Assembly of Notables.
March:	Clash between Calonne and the Notables.
8 April:	Calonne dismissed by King.
25 May:	Dissolution of first Assembly of Notables.

1788

5 July:	Brienne considers convoking Estates General.
16 August:	French government says it is bankrupt.
25 August:	Necker replaces Brienne as Minister of Finance.
6 November:	Second Assembly of Notables called by Necker to discuss Estates General.
27 December:	Necker announces that Third Estate representation will be doubled.

1789

24 January:	Estates General convoked for first time since 1614.
5 May:	Meeting of the Estates General.
28 May:	Third Estate begins to meet alone.
17 June:	Third Estate evolves into National Assembly.
20 June:	Tennis Court Oath.
24 June:	Some nobles and clergy join with the Third Estate.
9 July:	National Assembly becomes National Constituent Assembly.
11 July:	King dismisses Necker.

13 July:	National Guard formed in Paris.
14 July:	Fall of the Bastille.
4 August:	Highpoint of 'Great Fear'.
27 August:	National Assembly adopts *Declaration of the Rights of Man*.

1790

January:	Departments replace provinces.
19 May:	Abolition of nobility.
12 July:	Civil Constitution of the Clergy.
16 August:	Abolition of *parlements*.
September:	Fall of Necker.

1791

30 January:	Mirabeau elected President of the National Assembly.
14 June:	Le Chapelier Law passed banning trade unions.
20–25 June:	Flight to Varennes.
10 July:	Padua Circular.
July:	Voltaire's remains reburied in Pantheon.
27 August:	Declaration of Pillnitz.
13–14 September:	Louis accepts Constitution.
30 September:	End of National Constituent Assembly.
1 October:	Meeting of Legislative Assembly.
9 November:	*Emigrés* ordered to return to France.

1792

20 March:	Introduction of guillotine.
20 April:	France declares war on Austria.
5 July:	Legislative Assembly states that 'the fatherland is in danger'.
25 July:	Brunswick Manifesto.

10 August:	Arrest of the King.
22 August:	Royalist revolts in the Vendée, Brittany and Dauphiné.
3 September:	Fall of Verdun.
3–7 September:	September Massacres.
19 September:	End of Legislative Assembly.
21 September:	Inception of First French Republic.
3 December:	Louis XVI on trial.

1793

21 January:	Execution of Louis XVI.
11 March:	Revolutionary Tribunal set up in Paris.
6 April:	Establishment of Committee of Public Safety.
2 June:	Jacobins arrest Girondin deputies.
17 September:	Law of Suspects.
29 September:	Introduction of Maximum.
16 October:	Execution of Marie Antoinette.
23 December:	Defeat of Vendée rebels.

1794

February:	Pacification of Vendée.
5 April:	Execution of Danton and Desmoulins.
7 May:	Establishment of Supreme Being.
8 June:	Festival of Supreme Being.
26 June:	Austrians defeated at Battle of Fleurus.
27–28 July:	Arrest and execution of Robespierre; Thermidorian Reaction begins.
11 November:	Closure of Jacobin Club.

1795

| 31 May: | Revolutionary Tribunal closed. |
| 14 July: | *Marseillaise* introduced as French national anthem. |

| 22 August: | New constitution published. |
| 2 November: | Directory takes executive power. |

1796

| 10 May: | Battle of Lodi. |

1797

18 April:	Peace of Leoben.
4 September:	Fructidor coup.
17 October:	Treaty of Campo Formio.

1798

| 11 May: | Floréal coup against the left. |
| 21 July: | Battle of the Pyramids. |

1799

24 August:	Napoleon departs Egypt.
9 October:	Napoleon back in France.
9 November:	18 Brumaire coup – end of the Directory.
24 December:	Napoleon establishes Consulate.

Glossary

Ancien Régime   Name given to the socio-political system in France (and across Europe) prior to 1789; it was based on feudalism and tradition.

Aristocratic Reaction   Protest of the Second Estate against reforming intentions of the Crown 1787–89.

Assembly of Notables   Body of aristocrats which met in 1787 and 1788 to discuss issues of state with the King.

Cahiers   Grievance lists drawn up by members of all three estates in advance of the meeting of the Estates General.

Chouans   Name given to the primitive, bandit-style warriors in the Vendée.

Constituent Assembly   1789–91 session of the National Assembly beginning with the declaration of the Third Estate that it was the National Assembly.

Convention   Legislative body between birth of Republic in 1792 and Consulate in 1799.

Cult of Reason   Atheistic festival introduced by the Hébertists.

Dechristianisation   State-sponsored attack on Catholicism, which involved the destruction of buildings and monuments.

Enlightenment   Body of reformist and rational ideas that challenged tradition and 'old certainties' in the eighteenth century.

Estates General   Ancient legislative forum which met in 1789 for the first time since 1614.

Girondins   Moderate revolutionary faction led by Brissot; the Girondins took France into war in 1792.

Jacobins   Radical revolutionary faction led by Robespierre; they outmanoeuvred the Girondins in June 1793 and established a dictatorship.

Maximum   Law enacted in 1793 which fixed the level of prices and wages.

Legislative Assembly   Name given to the National Assembly prior to the Republic being declared (1791–92).

Levée en Masse   Decree of 1793 ordering conscription for all eligible males.

Parlements   Legislative bodies in Paris and the provinces that were dominated by the aristocracy.

Sans-culottes   Artisans and shopkeepers 'without breeches' who were a major influence on the Jacobins 1793–94.

Supreme Being   New deity introduced by Robespierre as part of the religious terror.

Bibliography and further reading

General

N. Aston, *The French Revolution 1789–1804* (London, Macmillan, 2004)

S. Bailey, *Reinterpreting the French Revolution: a Global-Historical Perspective* (Cambridge, Cambridge UP, 2002)

K.M. Baker, *Inventing the French Revolution* (Cambridge, Cambridge UP, 1990)

T.C.W. Blanning, *The Origins of the French Revolutionary Wars* (London, Longman, 1986)

J.F. Bosher, *The French Revolution* (London, Weidenfeld & Nicolson, 1989)

P. Campbell, *The Origins of the French Revolution* (London, Palgrave, 2006)

J. Censer & L. Hunt, *Liberty, Equality, Fraternity: Exploring the French Revolution* (Pennsylvania, Penn State Press, 2001)

A. Cobban, *A History of Modern France 1715–1799* (London, Penguin, 1965)

G. Comninel, *Rethinking the French Revolution* (London, Verso, 1990)

W. Doyle, *The Oxford History of the French Revolution* (Oxford, Oxford UP, 1991)

J. Egret, *The French Pre-Revolution, 1787–1788* (Chicago, Chicago UP, 1977)

A. Forrest, *The French Revolution* (Oxford, Blackwell, 1993)

J. Godechot, *France and the Atlantic Revolution* (London, Macmillan, 1965)

N. Hampson, *A Social History of the French Revolution* (London, Routledge, 1995)

C. Hibbert, *The French Revolution* (London, Penguin, 1982)

E.J. Hobsbawm, *The Age of Revolution* (London, Abacus, 1985)

C. Jones, *The Longman Companion to the French Revolution* (London, Longman, 1988)

P. Jones (ed.), *French Revolution in Social and Political Perspective* (London, Arnold, 1996)

G. Kates (ed.), *The French Revolution* (London, Routledge, 2005)

E. Kennedy, *A Cultural History of the French Revolution* (London, Yale UP, 1989)

G. Lewis, *The French Revolution* (London, Routledge, 1993)

R.R. Palmer, *Age of the Democratic Revolution: A Political History of Europe and America, 1760–1800,* Vols 1 & 2 (Princeton, Princeton UP, 1959)

N. Parker, *Portrayals of Revolution* (London, Harvester Wheatsheaf, 1990)

M. Philp, *The French Revolution and British Popular Politics* (Cambridge, Cambridge UP, 2002)

J.M. Roberts, *The French Revolution* (Oxford, Oxford UP, 1997)

G. Rudé, *Revolutionary Europe* (London, Fontana, 1986)

S. Schama, *Citizens* (London, Penguin, 1989)

R. Schechter, *The French Revolution: The Essential Readings* (Oxford, Blackwell, 2001)

D. Sutherland, *France 1789–1815* (London, Fontana, 1985)

J.M. Thompson, *The French Revolution* (New York, Oxford UP, 1969)

Primary sources

Exploring the French Revolution: *http://chnm.gmu.edu/revolution*

Internet Modern History Sourcebook: *http://www.fordham.edu/halsall/mod/modsbook.html*

L.W. Cowie (ed.), *The French Revolution, Documents and Debates* (London, Macmillan, 1987)

P.G. Dwyer, *The French Revolution and Napoleon: A Sourcebook* (London, Routledge, 2002)

I. Hampsher-Monk, *The Impact of the French Revolution: Texts from Britain in the 1790s* (Cambridge, Cambridge UP, 2005)

J. Hardman (ed.), *The French Revolution Sourcebook* (London, Arnold, 1999)

L. Mason & T. Rizzo (eds.), *The French Revolution: A Document Collection* (London, Houghton Mifflin, 1999)

J.H. Stewart, *A Documentary Survey of the French Revolution* (New York, Columbia UP, 1964)

1: The Old Regime

A. Farge, *Subversive Words: Public Opinion in Eighteenth-Century France* (Cambridge, Polity, 1994)

J.H. Shennan, *France before the Revolution* (London, Methuen, 1983)

A. de Tocquevillle, *The Ancien Régime* (London, J.M. Dent & Sons, 1988)

D. Van Kley ed., *The French Idea of Freedom: The Old Regime and the Declaration of Rights of 1789* (Stanford, Stanford UP, 1994)

2: Origins and causation

F. Aftalion, *The French Revolution: An Economic Interpretation* (Cambridge, Cambridge UP, 2008)

R. Darnton, *The Literary Underground of the Old Regime* (Cambridge, Harvard UP, 1982)

W. Doyle, *The Origins of the French Revolution* (Oxford, Oxford UP, 1985)

H. Dunthorne, *The Enlightenment* (London, History Association, 1991)

N. Hampson, *The Enlightenment* (London, Penguin, 1990)

B.F. Hyslop & B. Fry, *A Guide to the General Cahiers of 1789* (New York, Octagon, 1968)

G. Lefebvre, *The Coming of the French Revolution* (New York, Vintage, 1947)

R. Porter, *The Enlightenment* (Basingstoke, Macmillan, 1990)

M. Price, *The Fall of the French Monarchy: Louis XVI, Marie Antoinette and the Baron de Breteuil* (London, Macmillan, 2002)

M. Vovelle, *The Fall of the French Monarchy 1787–92* (Cambridge, Cambridge UP, 1984)

3: The year of revolution: 1789

J. Godechot, *The Taking of the Bastille* (London, Faber & Faber, 1970)

P. Jones, *The Peasantry in the French Revolution* (Cambridge, Cambridge UP, 1988)

G. Lefebvre, *The Great Fear of 1789: Rural Panic in Revolutionary France* (Princeton, Princeton UP, 1973)

4: The liberal revolution: 1790–92

M. Bouloiseau, *The Jacobin Republic 1792–1794* (Cambridge, Cambridge UP, 1984)

N. Hampson, *Prelude to Terror* (New York, Blackwell, 1988)

G. Lefebvre, *The French Revolution: from its Origins to 1793* (London, Routledge, 2001)

M. Vovelle, *The Fall of the French Monarchy 1787–92* (Cambridge, Cambridge UP, 1984)

M.J. Whittock, *The French Revolution 1789–94* (London, Hodder & Stoughton, 2001)

5: War and terror: 1792–94

D. Arasse, *The Guillotine and the Terror* (London, Penguin, 1991)

M. Bouloiseau, *The Jacobin Republic 1792–1794* (Cambridge, Cambridge UP, 1983)

G. Fife, *The Terror* (London, Portrait, 2004)

D. Greer, *The Incidence of the Terror during the French Revolution: A Statistical Interpretation* (Cambridge, MA, Harvard UP, 1935)

N. Hampson, *Danton* (New York, Holmes and Meier, 1978)

N. Hampson, *The Life and Opinions of Maximilien Robespierre* (Oxford, Blackwell, 1988)

D.P. Jordan, *The Revolutionary Career of Maximilien Robespierre* (Chicago, University of Chicago Press, 1989)

G. Rudé, *The Crowd in The French Revolution* (Oxford, Clarendon, 1959)

6: The Counter Revolution

H. Balzac, *The Chouans* (London, Penguin, 1972)

J. Godechot, *The Counter-Revolution: Doctrine and Action 1789–1804* (New York, Fertig, 1971)

J. Roberts, *The Counter-Revolution in France 1787–1830* (Princeton, Princeton UP, 1990)

C. Tilly, *The Vendée* (Cambridge, MA, Harvard UP, 1976)

7: The Thermidorian Reaction: 1794–95

G. Lefebvre, *The Thermidorians* (London, Routledge & Kegan Paul, 1965)

D. Woronoff, *The Thermidorian Regime and the Directory 1794–1799* (Cambridge, Cambridge UP, 1984)

8: The Directory: 1795–99

D. Woronoff, *The Thermidorian Regime and the Directory 1794–1799* (Cambridge, Cambridge UP, 1984)

9: Revolutionary historiography

A. Aulard, *The French Revolution: A Political History* (London, Fisher Unwin, 1910)

G. Best (ed.), *The Permanent Revolution* (London, Paladin, 1989)

E. Burke, *Reflections on the Revolution in France* (London, Penguin, 1986)

T. Carlyle, *The French Revolution* (London, Amalgamated Press, 1905)

A. Cobban, *The Social Interpretation of the French Revolution* (London, Cambridge UP, 1964)

V. Folkenflik (ed.), *Major Writings of Germaine de Staël* (Oxford, Columbia UP, 1987)

F. Furet, *Interpreting the French Revolution* (London, Cambridge UP, 1981)

H. Goldberg, *The Life of Jean Jaurès* (London, University of Wisconsin Press, 1968)

F. Guizot, *Historical Essays and Lectures* (London, University of Chicago Press, 1992)

J. Michelet, *History of the French Revolution* (London, Bohn, 1847)

F. Mignet, *History of the French Revolution* (London, Bell, 1913)

A. Soboul, *A Short History of the French Revolution* (London, University of California Press, 1984)

H. Taine, *The French Revolution*, 3 Vols (1878), at *http://oll.libertyfund. org/ToC/0178.php*

A. de Tocqueville, *Recollections* (Oxford, Transaction, 1987)

10: The French Revolution today

R. Gildea, *France since 1945* (Oxford, Oxford UP, 2002)

J. Hayward, *After the French Revolution* (London, Harvester Wheatsheaf, 1991)

Index